THE
ULTIMATE
BOUTIQUE
HANDBOOK

How to Start, Operate and Succeed
in the Brick and Mortar or
Mobile Retail Business

EMILY A. BENSON

ISBN: 978-0-692-95176-7

The Fashion Truck
40 Main Street
Westford, MA 01886

Book interior design, typesetting, and prepress production by Lisa Von De Linde, LisaVdesigns.com
Editing by Alisia Leavitt Media, AlisiaLeavittMedia.com

Table of Contents

PREFACE 7

INTRODUCTION 9

    Are You Ready for the Retail Lifestyle? 9

CHAPTER 1 | FIRST THINGS FIRST 11

    Do You Have What It Takes to Own a Boutique? 11

    Assessing Your Motivations Behind Opening a Boutique 12

CHAPTER 2 | MARKET 15

    Targeting Your Market 15

    Research Like Crazy 16

CHAPTER 3 | PRODUCTS 19

    Assortment Planning 19

    Depth vs. Breadth 20

    Basic and Fashion Items 20

    Everyone Needs Gifts 22

    Developing a Retail Pricing Structure 23

    Pricing Structure Example 24

    Initial Margin Math 24

    Practical Notes on Pricing 27

    Selling Through Inventory and Taking Markdowns 27

    Speaking of SALES 30

    Markdown Cadence 32

    Another Markdown Idea 32

    Running Sales and Promotions 33

    How Are You Going to Get Products? 34

    Markets and Showrooms 34

    Ordering for Opening Day 38

CHAPTER 4 | LOCATION SELECTION 39

The Traditional Retail Location: Can You Open a Brick and Mortar? 39

Going Mobile: Are You Ready for the Mobile Lifestyle? 42

Picking a Vehicle 44

What To Choose? Brick and Mortar or Mobile? 47

CHAPTER 5 | MONEY MATTERS 49

Initial Investment Planning 49

Initial Brick and Mortar Boutique Costs 50

Initial Mobile Boutique Costs 50

Ongoing Costs: Running a Brick and Mortar Boutique 52

Ongoing Costs: Running a Mobile Boutique 53

Profit is the Goal 54

And Speaking of Inventory 55

CHAPTER 6 | DESIGNING YOUR BOUTIQUE'S BRAND 57

Choosing a Name and Tagline 57

Developing Your Brand 58

Social Media 59

An Email List Made Easy 61

Building Your Website 61

Customers: Your Walking Advertisers 62

CHAPTER 7 | TAKING CARE OF BUSINESS 65

Registering Your Business 65

You Need Insurance 67

Equipment for Your Boutique 67

Point of Sale Systems and Credit Card Machines 68

CHAPTER 8 | BOUTIQUE DESIGN 71

Brick and Mortar Boutique Layout Models 74

Mobile Boutique Layout Models 76

Display Fixtures 79

Designing a Mobile Boutique 79

CHAPTER 9 | OPENING YOUR BOUTIQUE 83

Planning an Opening Event 83

Press Releases and Getting the Word Out 85

Your Opening Event 87

CHAPTER 10 | OPERATING YOUR BRICK AND MORTAR BOUTIQUE 89

Daily Operations 89

Community Relations 91

CHAPTER 11 | OPERATING YOUR MOBILE BOUTIQUE 93

You Need Power 93

Permits and Regulations 95

Developing a Schedule 95

The Most Obvious: The Ice Cream Truck Method 96

The Big Ones: Markets, Festivals, Shopping Events 98

Try Teaming Up: Partnership Events with Local Businesses 99

Focused Shopping: Private Parties 100

Mobile Boutique Scheduling Final Notes 105

Vehicle Maintenance 105

Frequently Asked Questions 106

CHAPTER 12 | WHAT NOW? 109

APPENDIX | HELPFUL WORKSHEETS 111

Define Your Target Market 112

Retail Pricing Worksheet 114

Brick and Mortar vs. Mobile Boutique Pros and Cons List 116

Where to Purchase Products 118

FINAL NOTES 122

Did You Enjoy This book? Great! Stay in Touch! 122

To my most influential mentors,
Carolyn, Dana, Ed, Dina and Bob, for inspiring
my passion for retail.

To Dad, Mom, Jill, and Joan, for supporting my dreams
and loving me unconditionally.

To Greg, my inspiration for writing this book, and
for reminding me everyday to Have Fun.

PREFACE

Thank you for purchasing this book! I am excited to compile a comprehensive and fun book about opening a boutique that is easy to read and inspiring at the same time. I've included many real life experiences from my time with large retailers and in my own boutiques. I hope to help you get ready to open your own store. It took me many years of planning before actually jumping out of corporate retail and into my own world as a boutique owner. I remember how l would agonize about where I would open, what exactly I would sell and how the heck I would figure it all out. I wish there was a book like this that existed! Now, I meet many people who feel like I felt and I encourage them to go for their dreams—what do you have to lose? Yes, running a store is a lot of work, but it's also extremely rewarding. Having a boss, living on set hours, worrying about submitting for vacation time... I don't miss those things. I have a whole new set of worries, but at the end of the day I am the ultimate determiner of my destiny, and that is way more exciting than being miserable working for someone else.

Remember, you only live once. Make it a life you are happy to live!

Emily

INTRODUCTION

Are You Ready for the Retail Lifestyle?

You love shopping, clothes, home goods or maybe specialty foods. You always have thought you would love to be in charge of running a store, from the buying to the designing of windows and selling to customers. When you travel, you seek out the small stores to shop at and feel a little jealous of the people working there. Maybe you even have worked at the store or corporate retail level, always thinking how you would do things better, or differently, than your managers. You might even have a name for your store, an idea of what you would sell, or where it would be located. If all of this sounds like you, then you've got retailing on the brain! Congratulations on having a dream, now let's work on making it a reality! The goal of this book is to help you understand the ins and outs of running either a brick and mortar boutique or a mobile retail store! Startup concerns, social media needs and real life stories are all packed in here for you to create a business and a life you love.

CHAPTER ONE

FIRST THINGS FIRST

Do You Have What It Takes to Own a Boutique?

Have you ever wanted to start your own business? If you are self-motivated and have a love for products, owning your own boutique can be a great career choice for you. Not everyone is cut out for it though. How will you know? There are some key elements that a person should possess to have a chance at success in the boutique industry.

1. **Hard Worker:** You should be the type of person who won't stop working because the clock strikes 5 pm. The truth to owning a boutique is that you will always need to be on top of your business, whether you are in your boutique or not.

2. **Self-Motivated and Able to Make Quick Decisions:** You should have a sense of responsibility for what you have created and be obsessed with constantly driving your business forward. Being able to do that means making good decisions fast, and trusting that those are the right decisions for your business at that time.

3. **Open to New Ideas:** Owning a boutique is about bringing newness to your customers. You need to have a sense of urgency for forward thinking ideas, and be ready to track trends and stay on top of them.

4. **A People Person:** Customers are the lifeblood of your boutique! You have to be able to welcome, sell to, and

deal with people from all walks of life with patience, understanding and excitement. If people aren't your cup of tea, this could be a serious reason not to open a boutique. Think you can just hire sales associates to manage customer relationships? Think again. In a small business, customers want to know the owner and it's to your advantage to be the one who is face to face with customers as much as you can.

5. **Tech-Savvy:** In today's ever changing tech-centric world, you have to be able to be up to date on the latest social media applications, point of sale systems and website trends. Owning a boutique is as much about selling products as it is about marketing the heck out of those products. You need to know the ins and outs of marketing your store and items online.

Assessing Your Motivations Behind Opening a Boutique

Owning a boutique can seem very glamorous. But little do you know, walking into a cute shop, that all the items you see have been ordered, unpacked, inventoried, ticketed, hung and displayed. Besides the product needs, the trash needs to be taken out, the toilets cleaned, the mannequin outfits changed, the store displays flipped, the accounting done, the taxes paid. Every aspect of running a boutique ultimately is managed by its owner in one way or another. Try writing a list of what is motivating you to become a boutique owner and compare them to this list:

1. You love the business aspect of having a boutique: doing the math, marketing and networking.
2. You have a passion for great products—whether it's clothing, accessories or gifts. You get all the trend magazines and know the coolest items each season.
3. You love people; in fact, when you are in other stores, you often find yourself helping customers pick out what

looks good on them or the perfect present for their family member.

4. You want to help people enjoy shopping and love what they buy. Part of owning a boutique is being your customers' best friend when it comes to picking out what they want or need. Having the drive to be helpful, even with the pickiest of person, is going to get you far.

If you truly relate to the above motivations, owning a boutique is absolutely for you.

Here are a few things that should not be motivators or are misconceptions about owning a boutique:

1. You will have a new closet of things to wear.
   Truth: Items are for sale, not for you!
2. You think this is will be what makes you rich.
   Truth: Retail is not a get rich quick business.
3. You think you won't have to work weekends or holidays.
   Truth: You will.
4. You are just tired of working a 'real' job.
   Truth: Let's be clear, this is MORE than a 'real' job.
5. You love to shop and maybe even have a style blog- so this will be just like that.
   Truth: That's a great start, but it won't be that simple.
6. You worked in retail and now you are ready to be the boss.
   Truth: Sure, you may be more qualified then the average Joe, but please think long and hard. Maybe be the boss first, and then open a boutique in a few years.

Owning a boutique, whether it's brick and mortar or mobile, is not an easy job. If you are passionate and work really hard, then you have a chance at being successful. But, if you have any doubts or think it's going to be easy, maybe save your money or invest it in something else. Opening a boutique is way too much money to spend on something your aren't going to put your whole heart and energy into. ▨

BOUTIQUE NOTES:

CHAPTER TWO

MARKET

Targeting Your Market

Let's start at the beginning of your business planning process. You most likely have an image in your head of what your store might look like, a potential name and a good idea of what you want to sell. You'll want to first consider who the target market is for what you want to sell. Think of your target market as the center of your business. Once you figure the center out, you'll be able to build everything else around it!

Ask yourself, who is the target market that you'll be selling to? What does this mean exactly? In essence, it's a descriptive profile of the person you most want to be your customer. A detailed list of how old they are, where they live, what kind of job they have, how much money they have to spend and any other details that might help you zoom in on a customer profile. You can even put together an image board with photos and magazine cutouts of what this person looks like. When defining your target market, be as specific as you possibly can. Here are some examples:

> **EXAMPLE 1:** *Men, age 18-35, who have disposable income, like hip hop music, stay on top of street trends and will step out of the box for fashion.*

> **EXAMPLE 2:** *Women, age 25-45, who love shopping, have high-end taste and can afford it, and often attend charity functions and dress to impress.*

The first market example is for a men's street wear retail business, selling hats, t-shirts, sneakers and records. The second market example is for a women's name brand label retail business that sells high priced dresses, silk blouses, classy suits and statement jewelry.

Both ideas would work regardless of being in a truck or a brick and mortar store. The market is defined, and thus, the business can start to be built up around the focus on the customer at hand. The term market and customer become almost interchangeable.

Do you know your market well? Are they your friends? Do you see them in the city you live in? Get to know as much as you can about these people. You should know your market so well, you can draw them or spot them in a crowded room. As you build your business, the constant questions in your head should be, "Would my customer like this/buy this/shop here?" Making your target market happy, and thus spending money at your store, is the ultimate goal. If you are hazy about your target customer, or have multiple ideas about who your customer is, you will absolutely fail in pleasing them. Be focused. Be specific.

Research Like Crazy

Now that you have defined your market, you want to know absolutely everything about them, especially in regards to their shopping habits. Where does your customer shop regularly? Where do they shop for similar items to what you want to sell? Have you been to these stores? If not, go! Start to learn what your customer likes about them and why they are shopping there.

Competitive shopping sounds like a sport. But really, it is an important way to keep track of what is going on in the retail scene of your market. Take a trip to the stores your customer shops at. When you go to competition stores you want to think about keeping track of the store's styles and prices. What brands or styles seem to be their bestsellers?

What is the pricing structure they use? What's the most expensive item, and the least? Is there a price point many items seem to lie at or within? Visit these stores often to keep up with the new items they are bringing in, and even what might be on sale. Is there an item or color or size that dominates their sale section? Learn from that—it should give you insight with what doesn't work with your customer. Take notes, photos (be sneaky) and be obsessive about making sure that you know what's happening in these places. Even go so far as to ask the associates working what they are selling well!

REAL LIFE STORIES

When I worked for Henri Bendel in New York, it was an extremely exciting time. The company had decided to start producing a line of private label accessories. I was part of the team that got the opportunity to help design and market the launch of the line. Part of my job was to go out and research any and all competitors. I was tasked to see what specific products were part of their accessories assortment and what the price was. I looked online, went to stores and took lots of notes. With the research in hand, I compiled a fifty-page manual. We used it as a guide to develop the right range of products and a retail price structure for the new accessories line. Knowing what and how other retailers are doing in their assortment is important for every size of business.

Why the stress on what other stores are doing? Think about the money large or established retailers have to put into their businesses. Learn what you can from how large stores run, and think about what you can do better, where they might be lacking, or even how your price on a similar item can be better than theirs. It's to your benefit to competitive shop on a regular schedule, monthly or even bi-weekly. All businesses regularly check out the competition to keep tabs on the greater marketplace! ▨

BOUTIQUE NOTES:

CHAPTER THREE

PRODUCTS

Assortment Planning

When planning the assortment of products you are going to sell, you should have one goal in mind: To create an interesting variety within the store in order to entice a sense of curiosity that will compel your customers to buy. The most fun stores in the world focus on selling a wide array of styles, in a range of prices and end use. You want to do this, too!

At this stage of your business planning, you've decided your target market and competitively shopped similar stores. Now, it's time to figure out what you are going to sell. You probably have a pretty general idea in your head. Start to write down the products and put them into larger categories to help you layout the product assortment.

Let's go back to the examples of the two target markets and develop an assortment plan for the women's high-end store. We started with the idea of dresses, classy suits and statement jewelry. We can break that down into three departments: dresses, suits and jewelry. Now under those departments, let's list some items that we would be excited to sell to our target market:

ITEM	BASIC RETAIL PRICE	FASHION RETAIL PRICE
Dress	*$52*	*$109*
Necklace	*$25*	*$70*
Tops	*$42*	*$60*

After developing your list, start to think about the trends within the products and categories. Are you keeping up with the industry leaders on what is the "next big thing" for your market? For our women's high-end store, maybe large statement necklaces by a hot designer are what's being shown in major fashion magazines. Get some for your boutique! You want to make sure that in every category, you are always looking for new ways to bring "cool" into your assortment. This is a key factor to keep customers coming back for more. If they know you get new items every week, month, season, they will keep coming back looking for more.

Depth vs. Breadth

Developing your assortment and making these lists can start to trigger "how will I afford to buy all of this" thoughts. Don't freak out! As a shop owner, you will start to understand better what items you should buy in depth once you are up and running. When you first start ordering items, you'll want to think about the breadth of your assortment—having a wide scope of product, instead of depth in inventory. Because you are a boutique, customers will be satisfied with the explanation that you have small quantities of items. There is even an element of exclusivity when customers shop at a boutique. Figure out how you can spend your money smartly. Find vendors that have low purchase minimums on individual items and overall for total orders. These vendors will be a great resource for when you need to spend a couple of hundred dollars sprinkling in cool items to make your store look full and diverse.

Basic and Fashion Items

Thinking about items as "Basic" and "Fashion" is a good way to help make sure your assortment mix is diversified. You might want to only sell the coolest items, but customers will always see a need for a more basic version and look to you to buy it. In a fashion-forward shop, this might mean a solid color tank top, or a simple silver hoop earring. This mix of items is what will make your store more interesting, and also give you added income. Try to think about how basic and fashion can help sell each other. Say you have a woman's fashion tank top with very low cut armholes. Women might love the tank top, but may wonder how they wear can the style appropriately. Adding a basic stretchy jersey bandeau bra to sell with it, as a complete look, would be the perfect basic add-on. Having basic items is a great way to make incremental money and offer something that most customers need or want.

CHARACTERISTICS OF A BASIC ITEM:

1. A safe bet to sell
2. Priced to move quickly
3. Able to be sold in an array of colors

CHARACTERISTICS OF A FASHION ITEM:

1. Will sell to a younger or chicer buyer
2. Can garner a higher price than basics
3. Sold in the best special version

REAL LIFE STORIES

There are a few small colonial towns that have great downtown Main Street shopping districts near where I live and have my store. I try to take monthly trips to all of them to shop. On one of these trips, I ended up parking right in front of a new store that had opened in place of a recently closed gift shop. I noticed it right away because it had a bright and clean exterior with a modern looking logo. When I peeked through the huge front windows, I saw that it was a unisex store that only sold neutral color knit items: white, tan, gray T-shirts, leggings, sweaters. The whole store looked so blah. I had to force myself to go in. Still blah, and I learned, expensive. I wonder how long it will last before it succumbs to adding color, sparkle, or anything more interesting than the current assortment. Sometimes too much basic is a bad thing.

Everyone Needs Gifts

Whether it's a birthday, holiday swap event, anniversary or hostess gift, everyone needs a gift sometimes. Adding some gift items is a great way to add even more mix to the assortment. Most especially around the holidays, gifts are a necessary group of items for any store. Go back to the basics: think about price point, end use and give-ability. Feel free to check out seasonal gift guides from big box retailers and take cues on what they have decided are the best gifts of the season. Lastly, have point of sale wrap packaging ready to go, whether it's tissue, ribbon or boxes. People will ask for some kind of small bag, dust bag or box. Most people shopping for a gift want to be done with the wrapping process when they leave your store. Here are some ideas about how to build out your gift assortment by focusing on price point first and foremost:

UNDER $20 OR $30 GIFTS

1. Simplicity is key
2. Non-sized item
3. Neutral colors
4. Value for price

UNDER $50 GIFTS

1. More personalized item
2. Made from special materials
3. Could be a sized item, but a basic style

Developing a Retail Pricing Structure

In the business of retail, there is only one place to make money: from the products you sell. It is very important to realize this up front and take seriously what you buy and how you price it. Now that you have a good handle on what you want to sell, you should start to develop a pricing structure for these items that will ensure you become a profitable business.

If you underprice your items, you will end up hurting your bottom line. Customers might perceive your shop as a "cheap store," and unless that's what you are going for, you'll want to be making the most money off of your products possible.

Customers are willing to pay a premium if you have something they can't get somewhere else. However, if you overprice your items, you may suffer lower overall sales volume. To make up for the low turnover of items, you most likely will need to mark down items sooner so you can bring in new items faster. You'll always be putting items on sale, and teach customers to wait to by until an item goes on sale.

Find a balance in your price value relationship. You want to think about what retail price will allow people feel like they are getting good value from the items they are purchasing from you. Very often, customers will have the misconception that operating out of a truck is less expensive than a typical brick and mortar store; therefore, they are unconsciously unwilling to pay a premium. You know you have just as many costs as any other small business, but something about a truck setting will inevitably trigger odd responses in people about what they think they should pay for items.

Taking your notes from competitive shopping, you should have a good idea of what your market is willing to pay for products, from the more expensive fashion items to a lower priced basic model. Establishing a retail price structure for the total assortment is the next important step in your business planning. By deciding retail prices up front, you will be able to look for products at vendors that will make you a profit. Here's a quick example of retail prices that have been given to some of the products, noting the lowest price for a basic item, and for a fashion item, the highest price for the most luxe version of the item.

Pricing Structure Example

ITEM	BASIC RETAIL PRICE	FASHION RETAIL PRICE
Dress	$52	$109
Necklace	$25	$70
Tops	$42	$60

You should make a chart like this for all the items you plan to carry in your boutique. Knowing what you will charge for every item will inform your decisions on what you can afford to pay.

Initial Margin Math

Now that retail prices have been set, start to work backwards and figure out what you can pay for the wholesale cost to make a profit on every item. Initial margin is the difference between the retail price and the wholesale cost of an item, calculated as a percent. The higher your initial margin, the more profit. And the more room to markdown an item if it doesn't sell. Here is the initial margin formula:

$$\text{Initial Margin \%} = \frac{(\text{Retail Price} - \text{Wholesale Cost})}{\text{Retail Price}}$$

The very lowest initial margin percent you would want to get is a 50%. Ideally, all of your product will fall between a 60-70%+ initial margin. This is going to make you the most amount of profit, and give you room to markdown the price if it doesn't sell at the original ticketed price.

In my experience in the corporate retail world, I was always pushed to achieve the absolute highest initial margin possible. As long as the retail price does not feel too high, and the items feels like it's a good value, go for the highest initial margin you can get. Remember, selling items is the only way you make money owning a boutique.

For the lowest retail priced dress you can calculate the wholesale cost:

$$65\% = \frac{(\$40 - X)}{\$40} \qquad X = \$14$$

For the most basic dress, the wholesale cost would need to be around \$14 at a 65% margin.

For the highest retail priced dress you can calculate the wholesale cost:

$$65\% = \frac{(\$89 - X)}{\$89} \qquad X = \$34$$

For the highest retail priced dress, the wholesale cost could be up to \$34 at a 65% margin.

Now that you know the formula for calculating initial margin, you can use it on the entire list of products for your store! Use this basic/fashion format as a guide, a maximum/minimum scale. Having products that fall within this range is important to create more price variety within the assortment. As you grow your business, you should be able to discover if there is a "sweet spot" for specific items. For example, a dress that's wearable day to night and made of washer-friendly fabric can sell from \$52-58. That sweet spot is where you should focus the bulk of your buying, in both time sourcing and shelf space. The sweet spot becomes the core driver of your business and should be where you make the most amount of money because you are selling items at a 65% margin and a high volume.

If your goods are falling above 70%, and you consider the retail price to be acceptable within the scope of your competitive research, then go ahead and price away. Remember, with all your research in hand, and good instincts on what your target market is willing to pay, you should feel confident in pricing items to make a solid profit.

REAL LIFE STORIES

In the fall of 2014, I found an angora blend cowl neck poncho that I just loved for The Fashion Truck. I didn't love the wholesale cost at $28 though. Why would anyone pay $60+ for a knit square of fabric with no arms? I decided to buy 5 units, in 3 neutral colors, and price it at $58, a terrible 52% margin. It was on the floor on a Wednesday afternoon, and by Thursday at noon all 5 were gone (two women had purchased 2!). I immediately ordered 15 units more, and when they came in, priced them at $68 to see what happened. I sold the 15 out in 5 days and reordered more, this time going up to $72. This slowed sales a bit, but it was also nearing the end of the great New England Fall "sweater and boots" season. I realized what was working quickly and by maxing out the price, I made as much money as possible with that one style.

Practical Notes on Pricing

If you cannot get a high margin off an item, don't buy it to sell in your store. You are taking the risk that if it doesn't sell, you may lose money on it if you have to mark it down to a price close to cost.

You can always change prices! As a general rule, people at first tend to underprice the value of what is sold. Take a leap and start a bit higher than you think you should. You can make a little more money, and it will help you avoid customers thinking you are a "cheap store."

Once you see how customers react to price points, think about adjusting. If customers seem to like an item, but often put it back on the rack, perhaps the price is too high. If you are selling out at a faster rate that you initially expected, then consider ticketing at a slightly higher price. Instead of putting that item on "sale", just take the ticket off and replace it with the new price, whether it needs to go up or down.

Always double check against the competition! Shop local stores and national chains you know your customers are shopping. Sometimes a store might even have the same item. Decide if you think where your store lies on the playing field with the opposing store. Consider whether you should be the same price, less expensive (a better deal!) or more expensive (your merchandise is more high-end or for a more established customer).

Keep in mind that every item has a shelf life. You will need to take markdowns seasonally at the minimum.

Selling Through Inventory and Taking Markdowns

In the world of merchandising there is a saying that goes, "Maximize what works, minimize what doesn't." Seems like a no-brainer, right? But very seriously, this way of thinking should be your mantra as the merchant of your business. By repeating this daily, you'll start to realize where the points of success are, and when you are making mistakes.

This mantra applies directly to the flow of product through the sales floor, from when it arrives, to when it's gone. How quickly is an item selling? By applying this theory to every item in your store, you can guide your business to the height of profitability.

If an item is selling quickly, your first thought should be: "How can I make the most of this hot item?" Should I buy more in the same color, add it in another color, or in a print? Can I add another product that is similar, but a bit different? Is there an opportunity to add a few dollars to the ticket price and make a little more money? In how many ways can you maximize the success of the item? It is great to sell quickly, or sell out. But each time you sell out of an item, you have then missed the opportunity to sell even more of it. Having inventory in a hot item will maximize how much money you make! Think about how you can always stay on top of a hot item to keep the streak of success going!

On the flip side, what happens when an item doesn't sell quickly? You need to learn about WHY it's not selling:

- Is it too expensive? As the merchant of your business, you want to be constantly listening and observing all of your customers. Do you see them picking something up, looking at the price, then putting it down? Have you overheard your target market customer say anything about the price of an item? Listen, your customers will tell you!

- Is there an issue with the quality, fit or material? It will come up that an item just isn't quite right. Know how an item fits and feels when it arrives at your store. You want to tell the customer about any issues before they walk into a dressing room and realize that there is something off about the item. You should be an informed merchant and know what might be off about the item! Saying "It's not you, it's the item!" will allow a customer not to take it personally if a garment has fit or quality issues.

- Have you tried featuring the item with another complimentary item? Let's say you bought a bunch of fedoras for the summer and customers are hesitant about them. Find photos of ways celebrities or bloggers are styling fedoras with outfits to give your customers ideas on how to wear them. Post the photos on social media or create an inspiration board to hang near the item.

- Try moving it to a new spot or featuring it on a mannequin in your shop. This is another way you can help a customer to understand the item better! Perhaps you've brought a highly specialized product in, like a new skincare or makeup line. Having it near the cashwrap might be the best way to have conversations about it with customers. You can be right there to describe its benefits. The cashwrap is a great natural place to strike up conversation, so it's an easy way to sell without feeling like you have to put on your salesperson cap!

These are all just ideas! You'll want to do as much as you can before putting an item on sale. The most important takeaway when an item isn't selling is to learn WHY, and not repeat the WHY ever again.

REAL LIFE STORIES

In the summer of 2011, when I very first opened The Fashion Truck mobile boutique, I kept seeing one-shoulder dresses in *magazines. I found some cute ones from my vendors and ended up buying 2 styles for the store. One of the styles I had in 2 colors. As I watched women try them on, they just didn't quite work. The waist was too small and the bust too big. Or the bust was too small and the waist was too big. Other items that I bought from the vendors that made the one shoulder dresses were fitting and selling just fine! What I realized is that one shoulder dresses are a tough fit, since women's bodies are so varied in the waist and bust measurements. I ended up using the dresses as material for a kids' fashion class, because even after marking them down to $15 and letting them sit on the rack for 2 years, I still had 5 left! Lesson learned. I have never again bought one shoulder dresses for the store!*

Speaking of SALES

If you've ever been to a big retail store, you know that there is always a sale section. The sale section contains items that either didn't work, that the store bought too much of, or "one-offs," a size or color of a style that just has one left. Few items you buy for your store will ever sell out completely at full price, especially if you are buying multiple sizes of an item. The lifecycle of a product always includes "dying" via a sale period. One of the biggest arguments for having a 60-70% initial margin is so that you have room to mark items down. The trick to a good markdown cadence is to think about a customer's reaction to the difference in sale price from the original price. You know that you've had that "wow" moment when you find an item you love at 50% or even 70% off the regular price. Your brain thinks "what a deal" and you feel compelled to buy it. Let's talk about how we can use that same strategy to your advantage in your store.

The cadence of your markdowns is important. Just because an item is slow at first, or it's only sold half its quantity after some time, does not mean that you have to take a huge markdown right away. Establishing a cadence to markdowns will ensure that although you aren't making full initial margin on every unit, you are still making money on every unit. The big box retailers call each markdown a "hit". You want to take a maximum of 3 hits to any item you've decided should go on sale. Any more than 3 hits and it gets confusing and you risk losing money on an items. Three hits provide those substantial 'wow' discounts every customer loves. And because each item starts at a 60-70% initial margin you can afford to take 3 "wow" hits.

The first hit should always be substantial enough for a customer to purchase right away, if they may have been on the fence about purchasing the item when they saw it at the original price. You can decide what is right for your store, but 30% off on a first hit feels like a comfortable big drop. The second hit should be at 50% off the original price. For a small business, this should feel like a huge discount to the customer, and there should be little to no barrier to purchase. If an item is still hanging around at 50% off for awhile, go ahead and take one more hit and go as close to the wholesale cost as you feel comfortable without going below it. Once you go below cost, you are losing money. You can see that throughout this paragraph, "feel" was a key verb. You are free to decide and "feel'" what is right for your store, your products, your customers. Maybe you learn that your customers will automatically purchase at 50% off and you decide that will be your first hit, go for it! The final price should never be lower than cost... unless it's a terrible, awful item and you are willing to take that hit to your bottom line (it happens!) If you have to lose money on an item just to get rid of it and have the cash in your pocket, by all means go ahead. Just learn from that experience and that item, so you never repeat your mistake.

Markdown Cadence:

RETAIL PRICE	FIRST MARKDOWN	SECOND MARKDOWN	FINAL & LOWEST MARKDOWN
60-70% IMP	*30% off*	*50% off*	*Above cost, the lowest price you can go and still make money*

Let's apply the markdown theory to an example: 6 units of an item were purchased at a wholesale cost of $22. Based on the pricing structure, $68 was determined to be a good retail price, and so the initial margin percentage was 67.6%. This IMP gives plenty of wiggle room to mark this item down. Over the first two weeks of the item in the store, 3 units sold. Over the next two weeks, none sold. This is a good time to take the first markdown, and remember it should be a substantial amount off the original retail price, around 30% off. With this item, that means a $20 savings for the customer. Generally, this price drop will give a customer on the fence, enough of a push to go ahead and make the purchase. With this markdown, two more sell and the last one left is just lingering around the store. Here's where the choice needs to be made to either go deep on the next discount and go right to $28 or stay conservative and still make a good amount of money on the item and price at $38. How quick will it sell? Use that decision factor to make a choice.

EXAMPLE:

RETAIL PRICE	FIRST MARKDOWN	SECOND MARKDOWN	FINAL & LOWEST MARKDOWN	COST
$68	*$48*	*$38*	*$28*	*$22*

Another Markdown Idea

The easiest markdown strategy is to keep it simple and straightforward. It can be employed at the end of a quarter to liquidate seasonal merchandise. Perhaps it's the end of the winter season, and you want to get rid of all the winter accessories in store, like hats, gloves, and scarves. In this case, you could easily create a bucket for each category, place on a sale table and label at one flat price, i.e., scarves for $15, hats for $10, gloves for $5. This simple strategy can quickly create a sale space in your store that customers gravitate to. Uncomplicated pricing makes the purchase a no brainer and customers love the effortlessness that comes along with that.

REAL LIFE STORIES

In the winter of 2011, I got a very early spring shipment for a lightweight top in 3 colors. I had no way to sell it, so I ended up just storing it until I re-opened the truck. In April, while finally unpacking and hanging it, some of the embellishments started to pop off of the top. I was disappointed and realized that I was outside of the return window with the vendor. It was still a cute shirt, and so I decided to price it at $10 to make my money back (it cost $9.25) and warn customers about the issue. I sold out of all 3 colors in a week because it was such a cute shirt, at such a great deal, and customers were willing to spend only $10! I realized I had to cut my losses and although I didn't make money on the shirt, I at least paid myself back for it!

Running Sales and Promotions

Different than marking items down is running sales and promotions. There is no right time to run a sale, but when you feel like your revenue stream has been slowing down, it would be a great idea to run a sale to get more people through the door. People love a sale, and it's a quick and easy solution for when times are slow. You can choose to do a mid-season straight percent sale, for example, 15% off everything. Between seasons, it's best to do a higher percent off the older items, for example, 50% off winter styles.

Sometimes it's fun to do special promotions. Let's say it's close to Valentine's Day and you sell women's items. Doing a jewelry or accessories only sale will get men to come in and purchase a gift. Buy one, get one half off for jewelry and accessories can help you move through accessories items and help customers feel like they are getting a deal. Around big holidays, especially the day after Thanksgiving for Black Friday, are important times to run special promotions and advertise them in a big way. Typical high-frequency shopping times are perfect for you to capitalize on people being excited to shop. This is a chance to look at the big retailers and take inspiration from sales and promotions they are running. You are allowed to copy what they do if it works for your store. Track what promotions you run and when, so the next year you can do what worked or change what didn't.

How Are You Going to Get Products?

Now that you know what you want to sell, and have a pricing structure you feel comfortable with, you'll want to start sourcing products. You have all the ammunition to be able to confidently walk into a trade show or showroom and purchase armed and ready!

Trade Shows

Every quarter, trade shows happen. Trade shows are an easy way to see and purchase a lot of merchandise in a three-day shopping spree. Most vendors will attend a show in each region, every quarter, so it's best to pick the show that's closest to where you live and attend that one. Any merchandise you want to carry in your store will have a trade show, whether it's women's apparel or pet items. Use the Internet to do your research and ask small stores similar to you what shows they attend.

There are many benefits of attending a trade show. You can get most, if not all, of your seasonal shopping done at once. Having the chance to see items in person, will give you the advantage of knowing how the fabric looks and feels. And often you or a representative of the company try items on to see the drape and fit. If you need things immediately, there are opportunities to have items shipped the same week you get to see them at the show. Lastly, because shows happen quarterly, vendors will be addressing mainly one season. As the head buyer of your store, you'll be able to see the overall trends in style, material, and color, helping you form the look you want for your store for the upcoming season.

Before you attend a show, make sure to check to see what the credentials are. Most trade shows will ask you to bring business cards and your federal tax id number to register for entrance. After you've registered, you'll get a badge to that will allow you to shop all the wholesale sellers' booths. Once you are registered with a show, they should send you badges in the mail in advance of every show going forward.

When you are at the show, you should expect to be overwhelmed! Imagine an open-air mall with hundreds of stores you need to explore to find items for your store. Make sure you are armed with your retail pricing structure and inspirational photos from recent magazines. You'll want to have a basic plan for what you are planning to buy for that time period.

Each time you enter a vendor booth, there are a few things you need to know. First, and most importantly, you don't have to buy anything! Second, know that the booths are generally organized by delivery date. When you enter, introduce yourself and ask the vendor representative how the items are organized and what the minimum purchase order quantity is. The items on display should have tickets or tags on them with the wholesale cost and delivery date. The delivery date is never perfect- vendors can deliver up to a month before or after. Lastly, you have two choices if you like items and the prices. You can do what's called "taking notes", where you or the vendor will write style numbers and colors down, and it's not an official order. You can call or email them later to order. Please know, this doesn't guarantee that you will be able to order the item if you decide later you want it. If you love something and have the money in your plan to buy it, go ahead and order it! Take pictures of anything you order or take notes on; it will help you remember when a vendor eventually ships the item.

You won't usually need to pay for orders at the show. Just give the vendor a credit card number to keep on file for when items ship to you. A pro tip is to have the vendor give you a call or email before they charge and ship the item. That way, you can make sure that you are ready for the goods and have the money in your account to pay!

REAL LIFE STORIES

I go to the shows in New York and every once and a while I will bump up against a buyer from a store local to mine. (Everyone is required to wear a nametag that includes their store name and location!) Do I ever worry that we will end up buying the same style? No! Every buyer has a different vision for their store and understanding of their customers. There are moments when I will see a style that I can picture a specific customer wearing—and that customer is unique to my store. The best advice I can give is: be true to your store's vision and what you want it to be. Even if the store around the corner has the same style, it's rare if anyone would notice!

Shows for Apparel/Accessories and Gifts:

- **NEW YORK:** Fame, MODA, Accessories the Show, NY Gift Show

- **ATLANTA:** AmericasMart has multiple shows every month by category

- **DALLAS:** Market Center has multiple shows every month by category

- **CHICAGO:** StyleMax Apparel Show, other categories quarterly also

- **LAS VEGAS:** Magic, Project

Markets and Showrooms

When you can't make it to the trade show, or you need items in between, markets and showrooms are always open! Most of the vendors that are at the show have showrooms on each coast or have an online store you can shop from. In certain regions, an "almost always open" situation exists for cash and carry items. New York and Los Angeles have abundant resources for you to shop all the time. In both cities' famous Garment Districts, there are stores and markets to shop for clothing and jewelry meant for wholesale buyers only. Minimum purchase totals are applicable, and most places will require a business card and federal tax id to allow you to shop.

Markets/Showrooms That Are Always Open for Apparel/Accessories:

- **NEW YORK:** Stores on 6th Ave/Broadway/7th Ave between 30-40th Streets

- **ATLANTA**: AmericasMart Atlanta

- **DALLAS**: Dallas Market Center

- **CHICAGO**: The Merchandise Mart

- **LOS ANGELES**: San Pedro Mart, California Market Center, New Mart, Cooper Design Space, LA Mart

Ordering for Opening Day

When shopping and placing orders for your opening day, you'll want to time everything just right. You want to have merchandise start to arrive up to two weeks before the day you plan to open. Give yourself plenty of time to hang, steam and ticket every item. Be careful to not to order too much inventory; you need to think about the right balance of merchandise. You'll want to keep the quantities of inventory to a minimum at the onset. Measure your fixture space and make sure you can make the store look full. At the same time, be wary of over-ordering so you aren't stuck with items that might not work for your customer. The first year in business, you'll be slowly figuring out what works for your store and you want to be careful to save money for items that take off, so spend less money up front so you can react to what your customers are buying. Remember, you can always purchase more!

Overall, being the buyer for your store, you want to make sure you don't get in over your head. Don't feel like you have to fill up every space in your store with something. Make sure you absolutely love every single item that you buy so that if someday down the road you are still stuck with it, you will love it enough to give it as a gift or use it yourself! ▨

CHAPTER FOUR

LOCATION SELECTION

The Traditional Retail Location: Can You Open a Brick and Mortar?

Opening a tradition retail shop requires some serious research. Thinking clearly about the target market you've defined, ask yourself some questions as you start to consider a brick and mortar location:

- What town or city do you want your store to be in? Is it close to where you live or plan to live? Can you get there fast enough if there is a problem?

- What neighborhood or street is where your target market is?

- What other stores do you want to be near? Are they complimentary stores where your target market is already shopping?

- Is there any direct competition in walking distance that sells anything close to what you plan to sell?

- Do you need to be on a main street or is it a walkable area where you can be on a side street?

- Would a strip mall or shopping center be the right fit for the area you are considering?

- How much space do you realistically need? Remember, more space, more upfront cost in rent, fixtures and inventory. Can you start somewhere small and expand in a few years when your customer base has grown?

After considering all of these questions, do you have one or many locations you think might work? Go there. Sit outside, walk around and watch for as long as you can, as many days as you can. Start to understand the makeup of the people in the area and how they shop. Do you see your target market in the mix? Are they carrying shopping bags? From where? What's the general traffic like, pedestrian and cars? Is there plenty of parking available?

Still feeling good about the location you like? Great. Now it's time to do the hard work of finding an actual space for your shop. Walk the area and see if there are any "for lease or rent" signs up in windows. If there are, go into the neighboring shops and ask questions: How's the landlord here? Why did the last tenants move out? What kind of traffic do you get? Do you think this would be a good location for my concept?

You may have to wait and watch for a bit to be able to find the perfect location. But it's worth it. When you are relying on people coming to you, you really have to make sure that it's the perfect spot where you will be able to be profitable. Perhaps you work with a realtor to find the right space. Just make sure you understand what the realtor might get as payment from you for finding a space and helping you negotiate a deal. If you plan to work with a realtor, make sure to put this in your initial startup budget.

When you are at the point where you are ready to move on a space, make sure to negotiate the price or lease terms if you feel like you can. Starting any business requires you to nickel and dime to keep your costs as low as possible. Even if you can nudge the rent down $50, or manage to get a three-year lease instead of a 5-year lease, remember, it's worth it to ask for what will keep you more flexible and saving money. Before signing anything, make sure you read the entire lease. If you need an attorney's help, do not hesitate to hire one for a few hours to help you go over the language so you understand exactly what you are getting into.

REAL LIFE STORIES

I moved into my brick and mortar store in a split sharing space situation. I had the large, street facing front room, and the woman who had been in the space for the four years prior consolidated her gift shop into two back rooms. Customers had to come through my front door to get to her space, but it was a good fit and allowed us both to operate two small businesses under one roof. Two months after I moved in, the gift store owner decided she wanted to move on. She was on a month-to-month lease, and although this was something I was expecting in the long term, it caught me by surprise. I had imagined myself eventually taking over the back two rooms, but after only being open 60 days, it wasn't the ideal situation. My landlord presented me with the option of taking possession of the rooms for the same rent the gift shop owner was paying. It was January 1st, probably the worst time for a retailer to take on more costs. But, I really didn't want someone else moving back there and screwing up my vision for the store. I negotiated with my landlord, at one point even telling him to forget it; I'd rather not take on the additional space. I just couldn't justify the extra expense in my head! At that point, he asked me what I wanted to pay and I told him a quarter of what he wanted. He took it and that was when I knew he wanted me to have it all along. It was ideal for me, and overall, it would be easier in the long run for him to rent to one person. Not to mention, he wouldn't have to figure out how to sell two random rooms in the middle of a very snowy January.

Moving into a brick and mortar store gives you incredible roots in the community around you. Whether it's the local chamber of commerce, or just the neighborhood association, you are now part of something bigger than you. It's a network to show what your store is all about and help grow your customer base. Having a traditional store also can afford you the ability to hire employees as you grow. A retail employee is easy to train and motivate, giving you some time, if you need, to have a life outside your business. Under the right circumstances, you won't need to be in the store to be making money.

Going Mobile:
Are You Ready for the Mobile Lifestyle?

Opening a mobile retail shop requires some serious determination. This option allows you travel directly to your customer, but can be the less glamorous option when opening a boutique. Ask yourself some questions if you are leaning towards the mobile retail option:

- Do you like to drive? Can you drive a big vehicle? Does the idea of driving a large vehicle on the highway, small streets or over bridges scare you?

- Do you have a place you can park your truck when you are not storing it? Will your neighbors be upset if they have to look at a truck in your driveway?

- Are you ready to do some serious groundwork to figure out where you can park to sell in your area? How will you handle people not taking you seriously, or saying no to you?

- What is the climate of the area you live in? Would you be able to drive all year round?

- Are you ok with the idea that you will have to work to schedule events to be able to make money? Are there events in your area you know will help you have a consistent revenue stream?

- Does changing weather bother you? Will you be ok in the rain, snow, hot sun or wind?

- How will you deal with seasonality? If you live in a climate with four seasons, what is your plan to deal with winters? Will you be ok if you have to work very hard for 8-9 months and then be off for 3-4?

Before purchasing a truck, you have to consider the realities of what a mobile lifestyle means! Running a mobile business isn't all glitz and glamour. Dealing with driving and maintaining a truck can be a hurdle. Also, being exposed to the elements day in and day out can take a toll on an individual trying to make it on his or her own in this business.

However, it is a great way for an entrepreneur to start a business if they live in an area where commercial spaces have high rent or are hard to find. If you love to travel and see new areas, they are great! Living in a climate that has good weather all year round is a benefit to running a mobile business. With all that said, the idea that your business can travel anywhere can be a huge advantage over a brick and mortar.

Picking a Vehicle

What kind of truck or trailer will you need? First, you need to ask yourself, how big do you want your store to be and how comfortable you are driving a large vehicle or trailer. Interior specifications are super important to think about. Will there be room for a tall person to stand up inside? How many people would you like to get inside at once? Limiting space means limiting sales, so find a happy medium of a size where you are comfortable driving, and customers are comfortable shopping.

Your budget should take into consideration the condition of the truck. The cost will depend on a combination of the mileage and year. Mileage on a truck over 100,000 will be cheaper; know that most trucks are made to go about 300,000 miles in their lifetime. The older the truck, the more repairs it will inevitably need. A truck over 15 years old is going to be much cheaper, but in the long term, you will end up paying more in repairs. If it's possible, have a mechanic you trust look at the vehicle before you purchase it. Generally, you will have to pay for a vehicle outright, as leases aren't usually available. Most banks or lending services won't give you a loan on a commercial vehicle if you are a startup business. Some lenders even have restrictions on the age of the vehicle.

If you decide to go mobile, there are a couple of options when it comes to creating a mobile shop, each with their own unique benefits and challenges.

Trailers

Converting a trailer or airstream is pretty popular amongst vintage wares sellers. Trailers are great because you never have to worry about the working parts- there are none! You will need a truck or SUV with a trailer hitch to be able to pull the trailer to each location, and once the trailer is in its spot, a place to park the truck or SUV. Most event organizers won't allow you to keep the truck at the event. Also, having a trailer may completely void you of being able to park curbside depending on your location. The biggest benefit to a trailer is the low price. You should be able to get one for less than $10,000.

Box Trucks and Stepvans

Box trucks and stepvans often get confused, because they both have a boxy shape. A box truck has a defined cab and chassis; they are separate and while sometimes there is a small crawl space between the front and back, more often there isn't. A box truck is higher off the ground, especially in the back space, so stairs going in to a shop may be steep. Be careful to check the interior height on a box truck because they often are short, less than six feet tall. Driving a box truck will take some time to get used to because the height of the front and back are different- so you have to be very aware of the height of the box behind you. A box truck also will look less like a mobile shop, because the overwhelming majority of food trucks are in stepvans. Most often, a person would choose to open their shop in a box truck because of the low cost for an all-in-one situation. The cost of box trucks are generally between $3,000-$13,000 depending on condition.

Stepvans are the trucks that major package delivery services use. Long and built as one piece, they are bread delivery trucks, snack chip trucks and linen service trucks. Stepvans are built for people going in and out of the back space from the front cab area, which is probably the main reason that food trucks were built in them. They have good interior space and a low to the ground profile. Stepvans are easy to wrap or paint with graphics, and drive much like a car, albeit much longer. When looking for a stepvan, the size will always be referred to in the length of the back space, not including the front cab. So a 14 foot stepvan means that the back useable space is 14 feet long. A 12 footer is the smallest you can get, 20 feet the longest. The front cab space is usually about 10 feet long, so add that to the back and you'll get the total length of the truck. The cost on a stepvan will run on the higher than a box truck, depending on the length and condition, you can get one for $6,000-$30,000.

Recreational Vehicles

RVs are another option for opening your mobile shop that will give you a half painted canvas you can build upon. Because RVs are already meant for people to go in and out, and spend time in, they are a good option if you have less money for interior redesign. You won't need to worry about building walls, ceilings or floors if the RV you want has them in good condition. Making an RV look like a mobile shop will take some imagination and some serious exterior graphics and a paint job. You'll want to get customers' heads out off the idea that people are sleeping and eating dinner inside and excited about it being a great shopping space! The working parts of an RV, like the bathroom and kitchen, will need to be addressed also so that you can have what you need, and remove what you don't. Because RVs are so built out, they will run you on the more expensive end of the spectrum, around $10,000-$30,000 depending on the condition.

Use your imagination to choose a vehicle. If you see a truck that you think will work and isn't one listed above, go ahead and try to use it! As long as there is space to have people buy merchandise from you in a comfortable and fun way, you can make it work!

Myths About Mobile Retail

Starting a mobile retail business can be an amazing alternative to opening a brick and mortar store. There are, however, some misconceptions about opening a mobile retail boutique that should be addressed.

1. **Running a mobile boutique is easy:** If you think that by choosing mobile is going to be easier, you are wrong. It is still a fairly new concept in the United States. There will

be people that will not get what you are doing and say "no" to something you need or just plain don't understand what you are doing.

2. **Mobile boutiques compete with brick and mortar stores:** Not true at all! Just like food trucks are to restaurants, if you have a great product, there is no issue with being competition.

3. **Mobile boutiques don't have to pay rent:** Technically yes, but they have many ongoing costs like gas, repairs and event fees. Some event fees are so high, they can compare to a rent payment. If you do a recurring event, say weekly, and it's $200 a week. That's at least $800 just in event fees per month. That is comparable to rent in some parts of the country.

4. **Mobile boutiques can just drive around and park:** No, this is not true. First, there is a space issue. Is there room to park on the street? Second, there are permit issues. Is it legal to park where you want? And third, there are customer issues. A mobile boutique owner can not rely on finding a random spot, tweeting a location and getting customers to come running. That is just not realistic or a consistent way to have income. (See later in the book where mobile boutique scheduling is discussed at length.)

What To Choose? Brick and Mortar or Mobile?

Since mobile retailing has taken off, there has been quite the debate about what option is better, cheaper and the 'right' choice. There is no right choice! At the end of this book, there is a worksheet where you can list out the pros and cons for you and your business. Taking into account startup costs, location, your current schedule and rent costs in your area are all serious considerations. You may have a 9-5 job and want to start a business on your off time. A mobile shop might be right for you since you can work nights and weekends. If your income relies on night and weekend hours right now, you might want to start with a brick and mortar store, where you can be open during the day and have an employee to cover times you can't be there. The idea that mobile is less expensive than brick and mortar depends entirely on the area you live. You may be able to find a spot where your rent is less than $1,000 a month. Your startup costs in that situation would be way cheaper than buying a vehicle. Or perhaps you don't live close to anywhere with an affordable brick and mortar space with good traffic at a reasonable price. Mobile may be the right choice so you can go to your customer without with required monthly rent expense. There is a lot to think about, and there is not one right answer. Keep reading, and hopefully by the end of this book, you'll feel confident about what choice is right for you! ▨

BOUTIQUE NOTES:

CHAPTER FIVE

MONEY MATTERS

Whether or not finances, math or accounting come naturally to you, the truth of running a business is that you need to know what's going on. Even if you have the money to afford an accountant, it is still important that you know where your money is coming from and going to. In this section, we'll go through initial start up costs, ongoing costs, managing money for inventory and some overall tips on how to run a financially healthy business.

Initial Investment Planning

It's pretty obvious that you'll need an initial investment to start your retail business. How much you need is dependent on how what kind of store you plan to open and how lavishly you want to outfit your boutique. From the last section, you should have somewhat of an idea if you want to go brick and mortar or mobile. It's important to remind you that the below numbers are estimates. It could be possible to spend less money, or more. Don't think because you don't have $60,000 you can't open a boutique. Good research, negotiating deals and some serious DIY can go a long way! Here's a basic outline of initial costs for a brick and mortar versus a mobile boutique.

Initial Brick and Mortar Boutique Costs

ITEM	COST ESTIMATE
Store Rent—First, Last and Security	$1,800–$12,000****
Interior Renovations	$1,000–$3,000
Interior Fixtures	$2,000–$5,000
Exterior Paint and Signage	$1,000–$3,500
Inventory	$5,000–$10,000**
Liability Insurance and Workers' Compensation Insurance	$400–$1,000
Point of Sale System	$0–$2,000***
Website Set Up	$0–$1,000***
Legal Set Up (if needed)	$0–$1,000
Cash On Hand	$500–$1,000 (+)
Total Estimated Cost:	**$11,700–$39,500**

Initial Mobile Boutique Costs

ITEM	COST ESTIMATE
Vehicle Purchase Including Taxes and Registration	$10,000–$25,000*
Vehicle Interior Renovations	$1,000–$3,000
Vehicle Work and Generator	$2,000–$5,000
Vehicle Exterior Paint/Graphics	$1,000–$3,500
Inventory	$5,000–$10,000**
Commercial Liability Insurance	$400–$900
Commercial Automobile Insurance	$1,000–$6,000
Point of Sale System	$0–$2,000***
Vendor Fees (for Events)	$1,000–$3,000
Website Set Up	$0–$1,000***
Legal Set Up (if needed)	$0–$1,000***
Cash On Hand	$500–$1,000 (+)
Total Estimated Cost:	**$22,395–$61,400**

*Note on buying a vehicle: If there is any place to spend some extra money, it's in the cost of purchasing a reliable vehicle that's in good shape. You really want to be sure it's a well running vehicle with a clean title and low miles. Remember, if you pay less up front, you'll surely pay more down the road in repairs, towing and maintenance.

**Inventory estimates for both stores are listed as equal. Regardless of the kind of store you decide to open, you'll want it to look robust with a variety of merchandise upon opening.

***The least expensive version of any retail startup model includes some things for free. Setting up your own free website, not using legal services and not buying into a fancy point of sale system right away can save you a good chunk of money. You can also enlist friends and family to help on renovation, or DIY as much as you can.

****There are rents available as low as $600 a month to as much as $4,000 a month, depending on the area. Research as much as you can for a great location that has good foot traffic. If you need to take a smaller space at first, do what you can afford. You can always grow into a bigger space or add a location in the future if and when business is booming!

The benefit to a mobile boutique is that you own the vehicle and could sell it if you decide you want or need to do that. With a store, you have a lower up front cost, but are locked into a lease term and over that term will need to potentially pay more over time if rent increases. Let's look at some estimated ongoing costs now.

Ongoing Costs:
Running a Brick and Mortar Boutique

ITEM	COST ESTIMATE
Rent	$600–$4,000 per month
Utilities: Electricity, Gas, Other	$100–$1,000 per month
Credit Card Fees (See Equipment Section for more details)	Based on Sales, 1.75–2.75% of each transaction
Commercial Liability Insurance and Workers' Compensation Insurance	$400–$700 per year
Taxes	25–33% of Profit
Travel Costs to Buy Inventory (Flight, Hotel, Meals)	$300–$2,000 per year
Shopping Bags/Tissue/Merchandise Tags	$100–$200 per month
Cleaning Supplies	$20–$60 per month
Marketing Materials: Business Cards, Fliers	$20–$100 per month
Sales Staff	Minimum Wage or more
Website Hosting Fees	$10–$100 per month
Storage or Office Rent	Varies by city
Accountant/PR Firm/Attorney	$50–$300 per hour for services
Banking Fees	$10–$50 depending on bank program
Loan Repayment	If applicable to your situation

Ongoing Costs:
Running a Mobile Boutique

ITEM	COST ESTIMATE
Vehicle Gas	$100–$175 to fill up
Generator Gas	$5–$10 to fill up
Office Supplies	$50–$300 per month
Credit Card Fees (See Equipment Section for more details)	Based on Sales, 1.75–2.75% of each transaction
Event Fees	$50–$500 per event
Commercial Liability Insurance	$400–$700 per year
Commercial Automobile Insurance	$1000–$7,000 per year
Vehicle Registration	$200 avg. per year (depends on State rates)
Vehicle Repairs/Maintenance	$500–$5,000 per year
Taxes	25–33% of Profit
Travel Costs to Buy Inventory (Flight, Hotel, Meals)	$300–$2,000 per year
Shopping Bags/Tissue/Merchandise Tags	$100–$200 per month
Cleaning Supplies	$20–$60 per month
Marketing Materials: Business Cards, Fliers	$20–$100 per month
Sales Staff or Driver	Minimum Wage or more
Website Hosting Fees	$10–$100 per month
Storage or Office Rent	Varies by city
Accountant/PR Firm/Attorney	$50–$300 per hour for services
Banking Fees	$10–$50 depending on bank program
Loan Repayment	If applicable to your situation

Whether you choose a brick and mortar or a mobile business, your ongoing costs will be fairly predictable once you are up and running. Ongoing costs should remain fairly steady each month or year. This will help you track of what needs to be paid for and when it needs to be paid so you can manage how you spend and save money.

REAL LIFE STORIES

When I first started my business, I was scared of the numbers part of running a business and overwhelmed by the idea that I probably couldn't afford an accountant right away. The creative, selling and marketing came very naturally to me, so why did this seem so hard. My father, who had been running his own businesses on and off for over 20 years, gave me very sage advice. He said, "You need to just keep an eye on where your money is at any given point. How much did you make? How much money do you need to spend on the things you need to run your business? How much is in your bank account? Just don't spend more money than you have, and you'll be ok." Sounds simple right? Well, this is the advice I've been using to run my business since day one. It's not intimidating, and it permitted me to understand what was happening with my finances. Thanks, Dad!

Profit is the Goal

The goal of every business is to make money! Here are some simple ideas to keep in mind when you are running your business that will encourage it to move in the direction of making a profit:

1. Maintain 60%-70% margin on all of your inventory purchases.
2. Watch expenses closely. Don't spend money if you don't have to.
3. Have a savings account and use it! Put away money for emergencies or slow times.
4. Set sales goals for each day, week or event.
5. Keep inventory levels small, so you can be constantly refreshing your assortment. Don't get stuck with loads of bad inventory!

And Speaking of Inventory

Inventory wasn't included in the ongoing cost section of this chapter because it really stands alone as its own cost. You'll need to manage your inventory costs using your sales rate as the guide. Each week you should look at how much you sold, what needs to be reordered and what you need to purchase as new inventory. If you have invested in a point of sale system, this is where it will be most beneficial to you. You can run reports that will show you what is selling and items that need to be reordered. It's just as easy to keep track by hand or in your head as you check people out if you can't afford a point of sale system.

As a general rule, you want to spend about 20-40% of your weekly revenue on ordering new inventory. Every business is different, but it's important always to be updating with new items to keep the assortment fresh, and reordering styles that are working. As discussed in the selling through inventory section, when you are selling more, you should be spending more on inventory. Heading into a slow time, like right after Christmas? Stop spending on inventory the week before Christmas, ensuring the store still looks full, but you aren't overspending heading into slow times. While you can't control gas or electricity prices, you can control how much money you spend on inventory, and it's wise to keep your inventory levels small enough that you aren't investing in styles you don't need or won't sell. ▨

BOUTIQUE NOTES:

CHAPTER SIX

DESIGNING YOUR BOUTIQUE'S BRAND

If you are a creative person, this chapter should be named "The Fun Stuff." Marketing your boutique is an enormously important key to its' success. Why does this chapter name include the word 'brand'? Well, because in this era of social media, you aren't just opening a boutique, you are creating a brand. A brand that customers will want to interact with in person and online. Your boutique isn't just a standalone store; it's an attitude, a set of colors, a certain "look." All of these things add up to make your brand unique and distinctive. This section will take you soup to nuts through everything you'll need to think about in developing a fantastic brand image for your new boutique.

Choosing a Name and Tagline

Maybe you have had a boutique name for years, or maybe you are having trouble coming up with something unique. (Please do not choose "Unique Boutique" after reading that line.) Perhaps you are thinking of something that rhymes, or is catchy or is a pun. Make sure it's a name you love and are proud to say many times a day! Do an extensive online search to make sure there isn't another store near you, or even in your state, that has the same name. You don't want to confuse customers or make them think you tried to copy what someone else had already established. On the flip side, you need to check that there isn't business set up as something you would never want to be confused with! Lastly, you want to see if your domain name is available to purchase so you can make your store name easily translate to a website. Once you have done your research and chosen a name, buy the web domain and set up all your social media accounts using this name, even if they stay deactivated while you get up and running.

Using a tagline can help more define your brand. "The look for less" or "the max for the minimum" are famous tag lines of discount retailers. Helping potential customers instantly understand what you are doing can make a difference in how quickly they walk through the door. Find one that works for your boutique and use it in all your marketing!

Developing Your Brand

What is going to set you apart as a small business? Your brand's overall look and feel is a huge component to help you shine. The goal in setting your brand up for success is building a professional looking and sounding brand that customers will want to engage with over and over again. Professional is the key word in the last sentence. You can spot a business that looks thrown together or done by hand. And most often, you probably don't want to spend money with them. If you really care about building a business, you will put serious time and money behind creating a look and feel to your brand that customers can take a quick glance and innately trust.

How does a professional look happen? First off, you will want to create an inspiration board of images and words that are what you want your brand to look and feel like. Whether it's photos of other boutiques, paintings, other businesses logos or inspiring phrases, take all of these and build a literal or virtual brand board. The board should have a clear vision of your brand's feeling and look. Second, seriously consider having a graphic designer create a logo for your business. You can use your board to send them for inspiration. Ask another small business that has a great logo who did theirs. Or go on Elance.com and find a designer that fits your budget. Remember, this is the logo that you will be using forever! It should look as good on a billboard as it does on your business card. Lastly, pick 3-4 brand colors and 1-3 brand fonts that you will use for marketing materials you create. They should be pulled straight from the inspiration board you created. Your board is what you will always go back to as a reference when you are first starting your business. It will ensure cohesion as you develop your brand image.

Consistent messaging to your customer is so important. Having a niche in your market is one way to do this. Perhaps your store is known for always having the best accessories, or great hostess gifts for under $20. When a customer needs a hostess gift, or a great accessory they will think of your boutique first. Go back to your product assortment and think about what you can be BEST at and how you plan to let your customers know.

In communications with your customers, whether they be in person or via social media, remember always to keep it professional. You can add your personal touch to an interaction, but be sure to keep your personal life out of the mix as much as you can. Perhaps you want to post a photo of your child's birthday party on social media. Unless you have a kids party supply store and you decorated with all products from your store at the party, then don't do it! There is a fine line between your business and your personal life. If you love posting photos of your daily life, then add a personal account for yourself to do that! It's all about using a personal touch, not your personal life to communicate with customers.

Social Media

Social media is a quickly growing, mostly free way to connect with your customers on a daily basis. Most social media sites are free and are a great marketing tool you can use from the minute you decide you are going to start a business. Updating all of these with new information and posts daily is important to the success of your business. These platforms are what customers are coming to find out more about your boutique. The chart below outlines how you should be leveraging these resources to promote your boutique business.

SOCIAL MEDIA PLATFORM	USE	WHAT TO SHARE
Facebook	Brand Blog, can double as a website	Post boutique schedule, photos of new products, talk to your fans.
Instagram	Brand Visual Dictionary	Post photos of products, events, customers. Post inspirational quotes and styles.
Twitter	Brand Voice	Show personality, have fun, re-tweet style/events that you like.
Pinterest	Brand Aesthetic Inspiration	Pin what inspires you, get ideas for displays, products.
YouTube	Brand Show	Use YouTube to post videos about your boutique, i.e., how to wear items.
LinkedIn	Professional History	Utilize to create a personal profile for you as a business owner. Write your professional history and post updates about what's new with your business.
Yelp	Business Info and Reviews	Create a profile for your boutique with photos, hours, location. Solicit customer reviews for your business and reply to them.
Google Plus	Search ranking and business info	Create a profile for your boutique with photos, hours, location. Solicit customer reviews and post updates. This will affect your Google search ranking so make sure it's updated often.

An Email List Made Easy

Having a big social media audience is great, but having a big email list is even better. People on your email list are engaged customers who have chosen to enroll in your email list. Your emails will directly hit their inbox so whether they choose to open your marketing message or not, they will still see your business name pop up. It's been proven that the majority of customers don't purchase on their first touch with your business. Keeping up with your mailing list will give you many chances to touch your customer the chances of buying from you increases.

How do you get your email list going? Keep an email sign up sheet near your cashwrap for customers to sign up on as they check out. Have a sign up button on your Facebook page and website. Ask customers when they are browsing if they'd like to be included on your email list for special discounts and news.

Once you have some names, sign up for an email service, like MailChimp, Emma or Constant Contact. Compare services to see which one might work for you. Many services are free until you hit a certain number of email subscribers, and then companies charge a small fee. Feel free to send out emails often, just don't over send. You know you get annoyed when a company sends you email every day! Keep customers informed of the big stuff- upcoming events, big new product shipments, sales, blog posts. Keep it simple, and customers will appreciate that you aren't trying to overwhelm them with your business.

Building Your Website

These days, if you don't have a website, you might as well not have a business. A website is a necessary to do for your boutique business. When you are preparing to launch the business, add in some time and money to buy a domain name and pay the monthly fee for a hosting service. There are plenty of free services like Weebly and Wix to build your basic information website. Once you upgrade to e-commerce on these kind of sites, you'll be charged a fee. Platforms that include e-commerce or that integrate inventory control are going to have higher start up costs. Check out Squarespace or Shopify. Most of these sites offer a 7- or 14-day trial period before you have to commit with a credit card. Explore a little and sign up for the trial to see if the design tools are easy for you to use. Everyone is different and will like a site based on how they think and build.

You are going to have to make a website choice eventually based on the start up plan for your business. Want to start off selling online, before you open a store? Great! Start with a platform that will allow you to do that at a low monthly cost. Don't want to spend a ton of time on the website and just need something basic that tells potential customers a little bit about your business? That's just fine too! Start with a free site that has the potential to upgrade in the future.

The option always exists to hire a web design firm to build your site. This is going to require you to spend anywhere between $500-$2,000, and depending on how the firm works, you might have to rely on them for future updates and maintenance. Make sure you know exactly what you are getting yourself into if you hire your website out!

Customers: Your Walking Advertisers

You've heard the term "customer service" on so many occasions. You might initially think of it as the desk in a store where you can make returns and complain about issues you may have had. But really, customer service is just how you treat your customers! From the moment you first make contact, you want their experience to be a positive one. You are the official host of your store! Imagine a time when you walked into a store and felt ignored. On the other hand, imagine when you felt welcome, excited and inspired. Which is a more desirable shopping experience? In which did you want to stay longer and maybe even spend money?

Creating an environment that customers enjoy is so important to your success. Customers want to feel appreciated and welcome. Your best advertising will always be word of mouth. If a customer has a great experience, you better believe that they will end up telling friends. A customer's endorsement is worth more than any ad you might put in the paper or on television!

Here are some ways to be an all-star, customer service focused store:

- You, as the owner, are the best salesperson in your business, the reason people are going to want to purchase from your store. Being outgoing, helpful and not pushy, are going to make customers feel comfortable to spend money. You can have the most beautiful store, high end or special products and the best location in town. But if customers walk in and don't feel excited or inspired to spend money, you'll be out of business fast. Be yourself and be excited— you can create a great atmosphere where people will want to come back over and over!

- When customers first enter, use inviting language. Say, "Welcome to (Your store name here)! Let me know if you have any questions." Let them look around for a minute or two and then perhaps ask if they are looking for anything in particular, or how their day is going. You'll be able to tell if someone wants to chit chat, or if they want to browse in quiet. After some time, you'll become a ninja customer reader and will anticipate the type of interaction each customer will need when they are in your shop. Be open and willing to help, or not.

- Each person that walks through your front door will be coming in with their own life baggage. You will be the recipient of that baggage, whether it's good or bad.

No matter what, the goal when interacting is to have each person feel good when they walk out the door. Hamburger chains say that the two most important parts of the hamburger are the first bite and the last bite. The idea that you want your customer to be satisfied and happy starts when they walk through the door, and ends when the door closes behind them.

- Remember regular customers. Know their names, their kid's or dog's name, the items they bought last time they came in and what they were used for. Perhaps a customer bought a dress for a wedding or a gift for their daughter. Go ahead and ask how it went! The more positive 'touches' you have with the customer will keep them coming back!

- Private clients can be amazing. The classic 80/20 rule applies to sales too. It's been said that 80% of your sales come from 20% of your customers. So who are your 20%? Find those top customers and treat them like gold. Give them extra discounts on big purchases, point out items you purchased and thought of them, send them holiday or birthday cards—make them feel extra special.

The goal in customer service is to have happy, repeat customers. Use the above tips, and you'll be off and running. ▨

CHAPTER SEVEN

TAKING CARE OF BUSINESS

Opening a business is one of the most exciting things you can do in life. However, there are a lot of not exciting things you have to make sure you have done so that you are legally set up and protected.

Registering Your Business

There are three places you will need to register your business—at the federal, state and local level. You most likely will want to do all levels at the same time, since depending on what stage you are in your business, you will need proof that you are registered for many situations pertaining to your business.

At the federal level, you will need an Employee Identification Number (EIN). The EIN is your registration as a business to the federal government, and every business needs one. Once you do this, the Internal Revenue System will know that you are running a business and you will need to file taxes on at least a yearly basis whether or not you are making any money. It's free to get an EIN, and you will need to know what kind of business set up you are planning on to do this.

In terms of setting up your type of business, you can choose to be a sole proprietor, a Limited Liability Corporation, an S-Corporation or a C-Corporation. Do your research and talk to your tax accountant to see what will work for you. Depending on your marital status and amount of dependents you claim, there might be benefits to being set up a certain way. The simplest thing to do is register as a Sole Proprietor (SP) at first, and then decide if you will need more structure. You can always change your business set up status to something else from Sole Proprietor. Starting as an SP will get you started quickly since there are no extra steps up front. If you are an SP, you will just need to file your taxes with a 1040ES form every year to show how much money you made as a "self employed" person. The only downside to being a SP is that if you were ever to be sued, your personal assets could be liable to the case situation. Again, if you have a complicated life situation with a mortgage, partner or children, it would be in your best interest to speak with a tax accountant or lawyer about what might be the best business set up for you.

After you get your EIN (you will get it on the spot!), you can then go to City Hall in the place where you will be operating out of, and get a business license there. Sometimes you will have to pay to do this, and it lets the city know that you are going to be doing business there. Most business licenses are valid for two to three years. Make sure you make a note of when your business license will need to be renewed.

Lastly, you will need to register with the state department of revenue and start filing sales tax forms for anything you sell that is taxable. Most of this information is now online; look for sales tax rate charts on what is taxable and at what rate. You will need to hang your "Sales and Use Tax Registration" certificate in your store in a place where customers can see it. Representatives from the state department of revenue have been known to go out and check local businesses, so make sure you are always in compliance with state laws.

You Need Insurance

Depending on the kind of store you have chosen to open, you will need different kinds of insurance. If you are opening a brick and mortar, you will just need liability insurance and workers compensation. In terms of liability, talk to your insurance agent about how much coverage you will need based on the value of your merchandise and fixtures. The best way to make sure you are covered is to assume that one day, the entire store could burn down or be stolen. If that ever were to happen, you need to protect yourself from losing money, so make sure you have enough money to be able to restart the store from scratch. Worker's compensation insurance is required in many states, even if you are the only employee of your business. It's not expensive and is worth it to have. If an employee ever did get hurt on the job, you would be covered for any expenses they might ask for. In an unpredictable world, it's good to be protected with insurance.

If you have a vehicle, your liability insurance will need to have a "rolling store" clause on it. Ask your agent, but it should cover the fact that you are a store in a vehicle and is an additional add-on to the main policy. Also, you'll need comprehensive and collision automobile insurance for your vehicle to even register it in most states. Make sure the entire cost of your vehicle is covered in case it ever is in an accident where it could be totaled. Finding an agent to cover your mobile boutique insurance policies might be tough, but keep calling until you find someone who is interested in what you are doing and wants to help!

Equipment for Your Boutique

As you prepare to open, you will need to obtain fixtures, office equipment and a credit card device. Make a list of everything you will possibly need and see what you can purchase and what you might need to design or have someone make for you. If you are opening at a brick and mortar location that is bare bones or refinishing a truck interior, you'll need to hire a contractor to help you build it out. Get many quotes before choosing to hire one company.

Even after the walls and lights are up, you'll need to get store fixtures. You have a couple of options for fixtures depending on the look you are going for. Ikea, for example, has some amazing shelving pieces that might work for your store. There are websites where you can purchase what is know as "slatwall," a traditional retail fixture. Slatwall is large, wall hung pieces of corrugated board that has grooves in it. Once installed on your walls, you can buy various types of metal hangers that can be moved around to create a pleasing design for what you sell. Slatwall gives you the flexibility to redesign your store based on seasonal items. For example, shorts would require a different height than pants. Slatwall would allow you to adjust the height of your hanging rod for bottoms to hold the length you need.

Perhaps you want more permanent fixtures or something that can stand alone in the middle of the store? Try store supply websites and Amazon to purchase these kinds of things. You will want to make sure they are commercial or industrial quality, so they hold up to the constant handling of customers moving items around on them. Another option would be to look for fixture stores in your area. You may be surprised to learn that you can get a used industrial rolling rack from a supply store near you. Or the local furniture thrift store has great shelving units you can refinish and save some money. Ask other boutiques if they have any tips on where to shop locally.

Point of Sale Systems and Credit Card Machines

Gone are the days of old time cash registers and sliding credit card machines with carbon paper! Everything is going digital and you are in a great position to be able to take advantage of this.

There are hundreds of point of sale systems out there that will print barcodes, track selling and inventory and run reports. These systems can run anywhere from $100 a month to $1,000+ for installation and then have a monthly fee. Do your research before signing up for any long-term contracts. Realistically, how big is your opening inventory? Are you able to run for a while without a true point of sale system? If you feel you need a system, there are some great options out there, including NCR Silver, Shopify and Vend. These will give you full capabilities to track inventory and take credit cards all in one place.

Perhaps the idea of a point of sale system is way too much for you as you start up. That's fine! Many small boutiques operate on a cash register and credit card machine. In choosing a credit card processor, please don't fall for any old processing company. Don't sign long term contracts, and don't pay over 3% for a swipe fee. Credit card processors will often charge a monthly fee, a swipe fee and a transaction fee. For example, you might pay $24.99 monthly to use the service, 2.75% every time you swipe a card and $.15 for a transaction. That will add up over time. Compare your options and see how low you can get all of these factors for.

In terms of actual equipment to swipe cards, again, everything has gone digital! Do you have a smartphone or tablet that has phone service or Internet access? Well then you can take credit cards anywhere you are. This new invention has seriously helped mobile retailers take off! Imagine being parked in a lot and swiping a credit card on your phone to have a customer pay for merchandise. This is now standard practice. To do this, all you usually need to do is download an app and order a swiper that plugs into your headphone jack or charging outlet. Some good choices for mobile credit card processors are called Intuit GoPayment and Square, both which work with Quickbooks accounting software, and PayPal Here. Do your research to figure out what will work best for what you need. But please, don't get suckered into paying an enormous retail fee for an old school credit card swiping machine. Invest in a tablet if need be; at least you can use it forever, and you own it! ▨

BOUTIQUE NOTES:

CHAPTER EIGHT

BOUTIQUE DESIGN

Key Elements of a Retail Store

There are traditional key elements that every retails store has. You want to be sure you consider all of these spaces and give them lots of thought in your interior design process. Whether you've decided to go mobile or brick and mortar, each of the elements below are important keys to your success in the layout of your space.

FRONT DOOR/ENTRANCE:

Make sure your entrance is welcoming and clean. When people walk through you want them to see a focal point that best represents your store. Do you have a stunning wreath on the door, or a welcome mat out front? Just like walking into a nice home, the exterior space of the store is so important to creating a good first impression on customers. Walk through your own front door and notice what you see first, second, third. Is it a pleasant experience? Change the focus weekly and seasonally as you get new items and the focus becomes different based on the timeframe.

FRONT AND FORWARD TABLE:

This is the first table or display people see when they walk in. Large retailers will use this table to place a key item on, something they believe is big for the season and they have bought a lot of. You can use in that way, or use it to show off a theme for the week or season. Having new items in the front of the store is important, especially for frequent shoppers to immediately get excited.

CASHWRAP:

Here is where you'll keep your register, bags and most likely will sit or stand most of the day when you don't have other work to be doing around to the store. It's your home base. Having a great cash wrap that's easy for you to use is important. You'll want it to be a solid flat space with enough room for both merchandise and a customer's personal belongings to rest on. It's a perfect place to include a clipboard for an email sign up sheet and business cards. Perhaps you even have enough space to include a shelf or space to sell small pick up items. Think of how the grocery store has magazines and candy in the checkout aisle; how can you mimic that in your store so people purchase a last minute item addition that makes you more money?

DRESSING ROOMS:

If you sell clothes, you will absolutely need to have dressing rooms. Having two to three rooms would be ideal, so even if you are busy, the wait isn't long for a customer. Have good mirrors inside the dressing room and one or two mirrors outside. Ample room for hooks to hang clothing and coats on is important. Add some chairs outside the dressing room for kids, friends or husbands to sit and wait. Think about the placement of your dressing room being near, or within the sightline of your cashwrap. Keeping an eye on customers trying on is key to helping them decide whether or not to make a purchase. Giving your opinion or just seeing how styles look on customers will be crucial for you and your business. Make sure dressing rooms are always clean, and there aren't left over items in them when a customer has completed their try-on session.

BACK OF THE SHOP/SALE AREA:

A classic space for sale items, the back of the shop can be designated just for that. Have this space look nice and organized so that although items may be on sale, they still maintain the great look of your store.

SITTING AREA/KIDS' AREA:

Is there space in your shop to include a small sitting area with comfortable chairs or a couch and magazines for adults? Often customers might have another adult in tow that isn't interested in shopping. Keeping them happy and entertained for as long as possible will help you get the sale from the customer that is excited to be there. The same theory works with kids. The more entertained they are in your store, the more comfortable parents will feel about having brought them and in turn stay longer. Think about having a small table and chairs with coloring books and crayons for kids to sit and color, especially near the dressing rooms. Having it near your dressing rooms will provide an activity for the kids while the parent has their own activity of trying on to do. Remember when you were a kid and got dragged along with your parents everywhere. Weren't your favorite places the ones with toys and games in the waiting area? Recreate that for your store and parents will be more interested in coming in and staying while their kids are "babysat" by your toy/coloring station.

Brick and Mortar Boutique Layout Models
SQUARE STORE LAYOUT

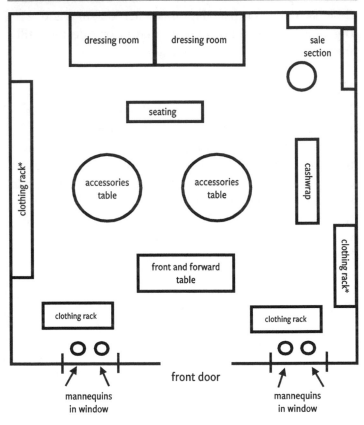

* When clothing racks are along a wall, they can run as a pole along the parallel length of the wall. Or to create more interest, you could choose to include some face outs, or waterfall style hangers to feature key items and outfits.

RECTANGULAR STORE LAYOUT

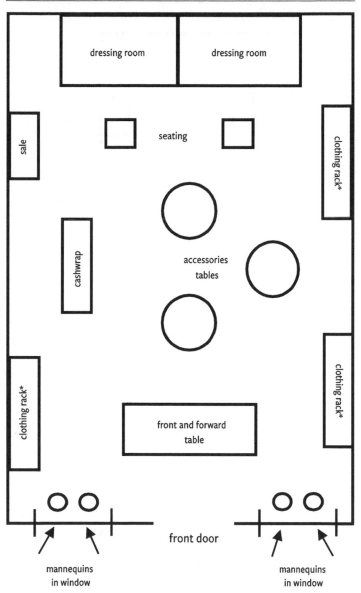

* When clothing racks are along a wall, they can run as a pole along the parallel length of the wall. Or to create more interest, you could choose to include some face outs, or waterfall style hangers to feature key items and outfits.

Mobile Boutique Layout Models
TRAILER LAYOUT

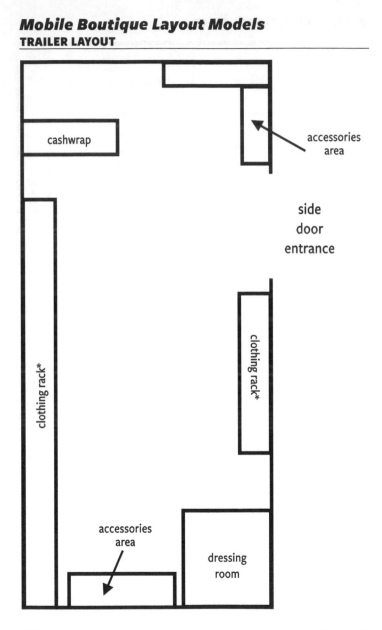

cashwrap

accessories area

side
door
entrance

clothing rack*

clothing rack*

accessories area

dressing room

* When clothing racks are along a wall, they can run as a pole along the parallel length of the wall. Or to create more interest, you could choose to include some face outs, or waterfall style hangers to feature key items and outfits.

STEPVAN OR BOX TRUCK LAYOUT

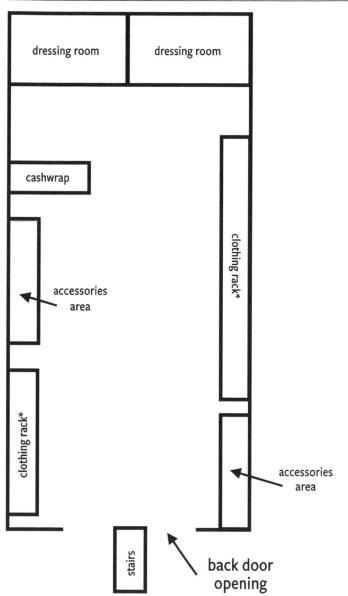

* When clothing racks are along a wall, they can run as a pole along the parallel length of the wall. Or to create more interest, you could choose to include some face outs, or waterfall style hangers to feature key items and outfits.

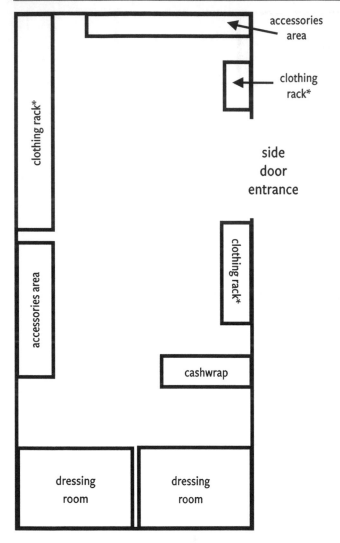

* When clothing racks are along a wall, they can run as a pole along the parallel length of the wall. Or to create more interest, you could choose to include some face outs, or waterfall style hangers to feature key items and outfits.

Display Fixtures

Having great displays is just as important as having great products. Depending on what you are selling, you want to make sure that you purchase the right fixtures to show off your goods. Start from the floor and go up. Think first about the big furniture: tables, racks and cabinets. As you layout the rooms, give plenty of room around the furniture for customers to walk. Three feet wide is the standard width for people to be able to feel like they have enough room to walk. Try different layouts and adjust the furniture until you find that it feels good to maneuver around the boutique.

After you have the furniture set, start to think about wall hung fixtures and accessory displays. Just laying accessories, like necklaces, out on tables looks unprofessional and messy. Purchase neck forms and bracelet holders; even ring and earring holders are available to make your display look professional. At the end of this book, there is a list of resources for you to purchase these items from.

Designing a Mobile Boutique

After you've purchased your vehicle, the exciting part of designing the interior to look like a boutique can start. You should have a general idea of how you want to configure the boutique. You want most fixtures to be up against the walls. Leave plenty of room for people to walk, look and pass each other in the center of the vehicle's open space.

In regards to the entrance, you'll have to figure out how to make it welcoming depending on the type of vehicle. If you have purchased a trailer or RV, they should have a built-in door to allow people to enter. In a stepvan or box truck situation, the back door opening will become the entrance if you build a set of stairs for people to walk up in on. Before you purchase a truck, take note of the back door, as there are two very different styles. The first is a big, latched door that rolls up into the truck, called a roll-up door. A roll-up door will generally be on a less expensive truck, and the grease from the hinges can drip on items. It's also very hard to put on any other kind of back door frame. The other style, called barn doors, are two doors that open like a double door on hinges and tend to be a more expensive purchase price truck. This style will give you a clean entrance look and will allow you to place another frame on the back entrance to have a sliding door or screen door added on. Building stairs, with a railing, will give you a safe entrance to have people use.

When building out the interior, consider mimicking a house. Use insulation and plywood to create the walls. Screw the fixtures into the sturdy walls to keep them stable while driving. In designing the fixtures, make sure everything is out on display. Using drawers or under glass showcases are an easy way to hide inventory, not something you want to be doing with the limited amount of space you have. Also consider having only a small section for backstock, as you want to have everything out for sale.

As for flooring, head to a flooring store and have them install commercial grade sheet laminate flooring. Using the strips of wood flooring for the home improvement store seems like a great do it yourself solution, but the movement of the vehicle will rip the seams of the strips apart and look messy after some drive time. You want durable flooring that will withstand foot traffic, including women wearing heels!

If you want to use glass in your design, try to use Plexiglass instead. Glass can very easily shatter while driving and make a huge mess. For mirrors, try using mirror tiles since they are less expensive and can be easily replaced if they break.

Overall, designing the interior of your mobile boutique should be unique, yet shopable. It should give customers plenty of space to move around, so they don't feel claustrophobic. And it should give you the ability to merchandise as many items as possible out on display for sale. The more of your assortment that is out, the more you money you have the potential to make.

REAL LIFE STORIES

When I first finished designing The Fashion Truck mobile boutique, I decided all the clothes should be in the front of the store. The first event I went to was a big market, and no one wanted to come in the truck, even women. When they did venture in, it was all the jewelry, in the back of the store, that caught their eyes. After seeing this, I immediately started unscrewing fixtures and replacing them on the walls so that the clothing and jewelry were more mixed together. Most especially adjusting so that there was jewelry right next to the front door. What I've realized over the years is that my target market of women LOVE jewelry. It doesn't matter what size they are or how they're feeling that week; women will always love to put on a little sparkle!

The outside of your truck is your roaming billboard. Make it look fantastic, with your logo big, bold and easy to read as you are cruising down the highway. To cover the exterior, there are a couple of options: a wrap or paint, or a combination of both. A wrap is a large print out that gets adhered to the body of the vehicle. You'll need to hire a graphic designer to measure and layout the print for the company that prints and applies the wrap. A full wrap, which covers the entire vehicle, would be done if you want a design all over. To do a full wrap might run upwards of $5,000–$8,000 depending on the size of the vehicle.

Depending on the condition of the paint job on the vehicle you purchase, you should consider painting, especially if you want it to be a pop color. Save some money by painting, and then have a small wrap or wraps for your logo and other text you need the vehicle to have. The paint/wrap combo would run between $2,000–$4,000, depending on how the size and amount of wraps you need. Plan about a week or so to get the exterior executed off site at the painter and wrap company.

Designing your mobile boutique will be a huge asset to your business. Making people feel comfortable in and around your vehicle should be your number one goal. Keep your design light, bright and classy, so there are no barriers in customers' minds to shop in your mobile boutique. ▨

CHAPTER NINE

OPENING YOUR BOUTIQUE

The time has come to show everyone your hard work and the new store! Your grand opening event should be a huge milestone, and you should celebrate it. There's work to be done in advance though, so you can relax and socialize during your party.

Planning an Opening Event

Whether you are in a store or truck, planning an opening event is a great way to kick off your business adventure. Once you have everything set, and you are about 2-4 weeks out from being able to open, you'll want to find a date that works for an opening event. If you are launching in a truck, it might be a good idea to find a local business or restaurant to hold your event at so that you'll have food and drinks available for guests.

Here's a checklist of what you'll want to think about to launch and promote your store for the opening event:

1. Create an opening event budget. Make sure to create a budget that will allow you to have a successful grand opening. Barter services if needed to make sure you can get every element you need to launch well.

2. Select a grand opening date as soon as you feel comfortable about having everything you need for opening your store. Advertise to customers, vendors, and staff as early as possible to create a buzz about your opening event!

3. Check local government rules about signage, balloons, or other promotional materials that you plan to use for advertising. Some communities have regulations, and permits may be required to have what you'd like.

4. Advertise to local businesses. Send out special coupons to local businesses. Networking is a great way to spread the word about your new boutique. Think about having a soft opening for other business owners the night before your event to get a sneak peek of the store.

5. Create customer loyalty from the day one. Offer special incentives for returning customers who shopped prior to the grand opening. If a customer brings in a receipt dated prior to the grand opening date, give the customer a special prize or discount for being a loyal customer. On the flip side, you can offer a discount for a future date. For everyone that makes a purchase, give them a coupon for a percentage off when they come back in the next month or two.

6. Have plenty of staff on hand. Make sure your sales staff is fully knowledgeable about the location of products, store hours, and store layout.

7. No waiting at registers. Plan for crowds to come and buy. Have all the registers open and ready to go!

8. Network with businesses around you. Once you have your date picked you can work with local business swap fliers in advance of the event. Local takeout restaurants can give away fliers with each order in exchange for giving out their fliers to your customers.

9. Contact local government and the Mayors office and request they participate in the ribbon cutting ceremony.

Politicians love to make public appearances for local business, and you should invite as many as possible.

10. Contact local newspapers and talk to the editor to inform them about your new boutique opening in the community. Highlight the benefits that your company will bring by either providing a needed service or jobs to the community.

11. Invite local high school marching band to perform at the grand opening. A small donation to the school band program can help with goodwill for the community. Present a donation check at ribbon cutting ceremony so community leaders and newspapers can hear of your good deeds.

12. Have local artists or designers that you carry come to the event. Perhaps set up a booth for them inside the store or in a window display creating custom goods for attendees.

13. Hire a photographer to commemorate the event. You will be so busy running around that it's great to have someone in charge of documenting the night. You can then use the photos on social media and for future events.

14. Set up a red carpet and step and repeat outside the store. Put your logo all over it and have attendees take red carpet photos and post on social media, with a custom hashtag for the event.

Press Releases and Getting the Word Out

Who ever said you need to hire a public relations firm or agent to help you get the word out? On a start up budget, publicizing your new boutique and opening event is absolutely something you can handle on your own. You'll need to write a press release and know the local press outlets to target it to. Think about sending out press releases any time a new big product line hits the store, or a huge sale or guest appearance. Anything that you want to get publicized can have a release sent out for it.

First, do your research on the local press outlets, whether it is small publications or larger newspapers and magazines.

forget television! Local stations, even if they are public ~~ss~~, should want to cover something like the opening of ~~r~~ boutique. Look on social media and newsstands at local ~~grocery~~ stores to find out what the media scene looks like. Make a comprehensive list of the media outlets you'd like to send your press release to. When making your list, double check that the media source covers the topic or location space you exist in. Ensuring that your event is relevant to the outlet will give it a better chance to get covered, and less of a chance it will be thrown out. As for the timing of your press release, make sure you are about two to three weeks out from your opening event. This will ensure plenty of time to get exposure before your event to advertise it, and coverage from a reporter during your event.

Writing a press release sounds daunting, but don't let it scare you! A press release is meant to give a reporter all the information they need in one page. Pretend you are writing the story yourself! Reporters get many press releases and emails a day, so you want to not only stand out but also basically write the article for them. This will make them more excited to use what you give them.

Start with your contact information in the header and a date for when the information can be used for an article. Make sure to include a contact email and phone number. Journalists may want to call you directly if they think it will be a quicker way to get information. Include a catchy title, perhaps one that could even be used in the actual title of the article. You want to persuade this journalist to copy your press release as much as they can so it's not only easier for them to publish, but gets you an article! Doing the work for them is key to getting your press release information published.

Now on to the meat of the release. Here's where you want to address "the five W's" of your event. The five are: who is involved, what is going on, where is it happening, why is it happening and when is it happening. Seems simple, right? Perhaps you even want to start in outline format with these as the topics of your outline to make it easier to write the full copy for the release.

Use short paragraphs to address each of the W's. Start with an overview of the event and each paragraph after that should go from most important detail to least. Make sure to give enough information without overwhelming. Use Associated Press style to write, so reporters don't have to redo what you send them. Include quotes from you about what it has taken for you to get the store open. Or ask a customer or vendor/artist if you can include a quote from them about how excited they are about the opening and your boutique. When you think you are done, read through the finished piece a couple of times, even read it out loud, to ensure you don't have mistakes, run on sentences, or misspelled words.

When sending out the written copy, include a photo, logo or some kind of image you think would be appropriate to accompany the story. Make sure the image is high resolution and in color. Even add copy for a caption. Remember, doing all the work for the journalist is the absolute key to ensuring your press release gets published. Reporters are overwhelmed and understaffed these days, so making it as easy as possible for your press release to be copied and pasted is so important.

Your Opening Event

You probably haven't gotten much sleep out of the pure excitement and amount of work you've put in to get to this step. Make sure you have plenty of food and drinks on hand to entertain the guests. Have a few employees there to help the checkout process. Pick out an amazing outfit for yourself and HAVE FUN! ▨

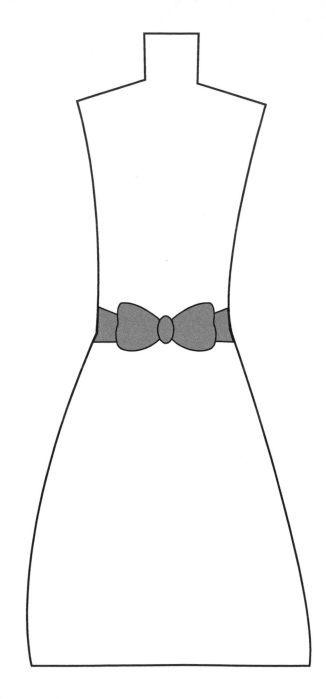

CHAPTER TEN

OPERATING YOUR BRICK AND MORTAR BOUTIQUE

Daily Operations

Each day when you open your store, it will be blissful. That said, there is a certain amount of complete obsession that is necessary for you to have as a boutique owner. Even on your days off, you'll have your brain on the business, whether it's updating social media or future planning. Your livelihood is dependent on the success of your business. When you meet other entrepreneurs or business owners, it's a guarantee that they will feel like their business is all consuming. It's equally exhausting and exhilarating. In any business, there are ups and downs. Keeping steady through the waves and staying on course is so important in realizing your dream of a successful boutique.

Having a fairly consistent schedule is one of the easiest ways to stay on track. Set your hours to be open at your store about 6-8 hours a day on 5-6 days of the week. Make sure you have your hours posted by the door and on all social media, including your Google+ page. Depending on your location in town, and your location in the world, you'll want to base your boutique hours on the businesses around you, the daylight hours, and the general traffic you observe.

Changing your hours each quarter might be needed based on these factors. For example, if your boutique is located in Boston, you might want to be open 11 pm – 7 pm during the spring, summer and fall. In the winter, you might change to 10 pm – 6 pm since it stays light until only around 4 pm. The earliest most boutiques open is 10 am, and some are open as late as 9 pm depending on the circumstances. Make sure your hours are workable and that during the first couple of months pay close attention to traffic to determine what hours of each day will be the most profitable.

Deciding to have employees is a step you will have to consider. Start slow with one or two people you can trust to work for you. Make sure they are friendly, are focused on selling, and well represent your brand. Train each employee as if they had to replace you for a week. They should know every in and out of the store: trash day, return policy, how to deal with difficult customers. It's a great idea to find people that you believe understand that they should do their absolute best in helping customers. But if in the end they can't, they should default to you for follow up.

No matter how many employees you choose to have, you are the owner of the store. You are your store's brand. You set the tone for the entire store and market everything to represent how special it is. You must always be available to your customers and show knowledge and excitement for the products you sell. Your customers will feel most comfortable with you and will want and expect you to be there all the time.

And it's exactly for this reason—you are your boutique's brand—that you should follow your own path as you run your store. Be up to date on the trends and latest styles, but don't ever compromise the integrity of your assortment to be like another store. Focus on why you wanted to open your boutique in the first place and be true to what you know your customers will love and buy. Customers will come to love and appreciate you and your products. They will take the time to shop with you because they know that you stand behind everything you sell.

Community Relations

If you have a brick and mortar boutique, it's important to be aware of what's going on in the community around you. Look at joining the local Chamber of Commerce or Business Association. Perhaps join a charity club like the Rotary or Lions Club. Networking with other business owners and leaders is an easy way to establish you as a part of the community. Designate an area in the store to hang posters for local plays, events or fundraisers. Maybe it's a spot in your front window or a bulletin board near the dressing room? Always say yes to people who come in asking to help publicize their event! Is one of the clubs hosting an event? Can you donate a gift card or set up a table at the event to tell people about your store? It's easy to be nice and get involved in helping your community.

Think outside the box with other ways to become a part of the community at large. Host events at your boutique with local groups. Bring in scout troops or kids organizations and speak to young people about being an entrepreneur and following your dreams. Maybe host a breakfast shopping event for the local women's group or playgroup parents? There is no limit to what you can open your space up as a gesture of goodwill. Get people in the door to see what makes you and your boutique special! Remember, to get people in the door, you will have to get out of the boutique and into the community! ▨

BOUTIQUE NOTES:

CHAPTER ELEVEN

OPERATING YOUR MOBILE BOUTIQUE

Being a mobile retailer requires some pretty different operations techniques than having a brick and mortar boutique. Let's go in depth about how to buy a generator, pick locations, research permitting in your area and maintain the condition of the truck.

You Need Power

If you are building out your mobile boutique yourself, you'll eventually get to the point you need power inside the truck. Whether it's lights, music or air conditioning, you can have everything you need by purchasing a generator.

Buying a generator is going to be a fairly large investment. Let's walk through exactly what you need so you are well educated on how to decide what kind to get. When looking at generators, know there are two kinds. There are industrial generators and inverter generators. Industrial generators are used on construction sites and are loud when at the full rated load level, generally 3,000 or more watts. "Full rated load" is when the electricity level being used by the generator is the maximum it can handle, so a 3,000-watt generator has enough items to power that the total wattage is at 2,900-3,000 watts. At this level, the gas in the generator will be used more quickly than if the generator is running at a lower load.

Inverter generators are the best for quiet applications. You will want to purchase an inverter generator for the fact that they are quiet, and most likely will cover what you need for wattage inside your truck, 2,000 watts or less. Having a quiet generator is important because if you are at an event with other vendors around, it is a huge faux pas to have a loud, smoky generator for your truck. Most mobile boutiques just place a small generator outside their truck near the front wheels. Because they can get away with a small generator, it's cheapest to just run an extension cord out to the generator.

To figure out how much wattage you need, you'll have to do some minor calculations. Look at the wattage of everything you need in the truck that requires power. Light bulbs, music machines, heaters all have wattages on them or their packaging. Add everything up to get the total wattage. Let's say you add everything and the total is 1,325 watts. Then a 2,000-watt generator will work perfectly for you. The "2000 watts" refers to the fully rated load for a generator. So at 1,325 watts, you could still add some items on if needed.

Let's say you want to add an air conditioner to your truck. This is something that will require some major wattage-between 3,500 and 5,000. At this point, you may want to talk to a shop that builds out food trucks to help you install this in your truck. You could also go a less expensive route and use a portable air conditioner. This would require a bit of extra electrical work, but would absolutely be a solution if you only need air conditioning a few times a year. Most inverter generators can be hooked together to increase the wattage if needed. For example, Honda has a great 2,000-watt inverter generator. With just a simple wire, you can hook two of them together and get 4,000 watts, which would cover a small portable generator. Unless you have a rooftop air conditioner with a built in generator, it's going to be hard to fully cool down a vehicle in the super hot weather. But providing some relief will make it easier for customers to shop and for you to sell. Figure out what works best for your climate and your budget.

Regardless of what generator you decide to purchase, you always want to read the owners manual. Learn how to change the oil and track how long the generator lasts on one full tank of gas.

Permits and Regulations

One of the most commonly asked questions about mobile retailing is, "Do you need a permit to do this?" That is a tough one to answer because there is no straightforward answer. It all depends on where you are and how you are operating.

Your best bet is to first check with local zoning boards and permitting offices to see if you fall under any existing regulations. Many cities have no idea what to do with mobile retailing yet, since it is still so new, and that makes the lines very blurry. You can take advantage of the blur and test your limits.

Often, if you are doing an event that's organized or on private property, you generally do not need any permits. You are most likely covered by the permits the event organizer obtained or that come with the private property. If the owner invited you, then you are fine to sell. Some states or towns have some kind of "Hawker/Peddler" permit or license. Basically, a hawker or peddler is someone that sells on the street, whether it's toys at a parade, or food from a cart. It would be in your interest to obtain one of these to cover yourself if it becomes necessary.

If there are mobile boutiques that exist in your area, email or call them to ask about what they have found out regarding permitting. At this time, most major and minor cities have a mobile boutique that may have the knowledge to help you.

Developing a Schedule

The most commonly asked question on a mobile retail boutique is, "So, do you just drive around all day and stop where you want?" No! This is a huge no! Driving around looking for random places to park is going to cause frustration and wasted gas money. You want to be developing a schedule of stop to park and sell. You've done thorough research on where and when your target market works, plays and shops. Now you need to place yourself in those places at those times! Developing a schedule with multiple stops per week will ensure that you have a constant income stream. The goal should be to create a workable schedule that will make you the most amount of money with the least amount of travel/effort. Make smart decisions about where to park, and in just a couple of hours, you'll be able to pull away with hundreds of dollars in revenue. Having consistent income should be a major factor in your choice of locations. Finding weekly events in your area is a key to unlocking steady cash flow. In this chapter, we'll talk about the ups and downs of scheduling events, and some of the best and most tested ways to build your schedule for maximum revenue.

The Most Obvious:
The Ice Cream Truck Method

The ice cream truck is the original version of the mobile retail industry. Driving around to neighborhoods and beaches with lots of kids selling as much ice cream treats as possible. This idea is most certainly where customers first relate the idea of selling from a truck from. The ring of a bell or music chiming outside an ice cream truck will bring kids running, but will it bring adults also? It might, but these days, social media is the new method of communicating with adult fans of your store. To make this method of selling work, you'll need to address a few key elements.

First, you'll want to identify high traffic areas where there is plenty of space for you to park along the sidewalk. That might mean paying a meter, or parking in a commercial space where you have 30 minutes to two hours to park. Or perhaps you work through your cities local parking department to block off space in advance. However you choose to do it, make sure that it's a safe spot, with good foot traffic and high visibility. Maybe it's outside a coffee shop or wine store. Park somewhere that people will be naturally walking to and from during the hours you plan to park.

Secondly, you'll need to advertise your exact location and hours to customers as a "Pop Up Location". Announce it through your social media outlets, put it on the Facebook pages of nearby businesses, maybe even let the local media know so they can help spread the word. Being tactful about planning this kind of stop can inevitably be helpful to get people to come out and shop. Of course, you will get the random passersby, but doing as much publicity as possible can go a long way to contribute to your sales total at the end of the day. Showing up at random times to random spots probably won't be worth it, so make sure you schedule and advertise your spot!

This method can be amazing for exploring new areas and hitting customers with the element of surprise. It can also be nice for you because you can use it to fill in times where you don't have any other spot to be—you have control over the date and time.

You want to be aware of any zoning regulations that might exist in your area. These rules are always going to depend on the city you are in. You can try calling City Hall or the Police department for rules and permits. They may say that they have no existing rules in place for what you do. Great! This opens up a whole world of parking for you! You do want to be considerate of other stores that are similar to yours though. Please don't park in front of a shop that sells the same items you do, unless you've asked the owner and made sure its ok.

Try out some spots with this method. See where works and where doesn't. Maybe no spots worked. This might not be the right method for you. But if you do find a spot that works, try to be there every week, or every other week. Make it a regular stop on your schedule and create a following of customers that will look for you each time you return.

The Big Ones:
Markets, Festivals, Shopping Events

Every area has events that are happening as you read this. They are organized by someone who is excited to promote small businesses and create destinations for people to shop those small businesses. You will want to be at these places with your mobile retail business!

Start your search online and look for large weekly, monthly, or yearly events in your area. They might be a Farmers' or Food Truck Market, an Art Walk, a Family/Girls Night Out or local shoppers event. Try to attend the event and see if your target market is there. If you see that this would be a good event for you, apply for it. Plan on paying between $25 and $500, depending on the size, for events. There might be an event for consistent income. If you find a successful event, be there often.

The best part of being a part of a large event is that there is built in traffic and advertising. You can advertise to your followers, but more importantly, the event is advertising to a larger audience of soon-to-be fans! Being a part of something bigger, especially when you are a new business, is going to add to your credibility as a business. This event is putting its stamp on what you are doing and saying you are cool enough to be invited to the event. If the event is something that happens regularly, this could be a perfect source of consistent income for your business.

Being part of a larger event has its obstacles. First off, you will have to be accepted to most. You'll want to have some professional looking photos of your set up and products to send to organizers, and a clear statement of purpose that is convincing to the board that may judge entry into the event. Next, you'll most likely need to pay an event fee. Set aside some money to be able to pay in advance for these events. Most events are rain or shine, so factoring in the issue of weather is always going to be a concern. Hopefully, you have gained entry to multiple weeks of a market or bigger event. Many market vendors have the saying, "It's all about the average," since week to week can vary based on weather or other outside factors. Make sure your assortment is different and on point, so you don't have to worry about any competition from other vendors. If you are reading this book, you should be well prepared to have a great assortment that is ready to be at any event and sell!

In conclusion, festivals, markets and any regularly scheduled event is surely something that you'll want to get into. Make sure that your target market is there and that you are ready to commit to the time and energy it will take to make these events a sure success.

Try Teaming Up:
Partnership Events with Local Businesses

One thing is for sure in the world of small business—owners stick together. Once you have your own business, you'll be surprised at what happens when you go out and talk about it. People will tell you about their businesses, or their friends, that you should network with. Learning from and working with other small business owners has many advantages. Converting those connections into events is an amazing opportunity.

You'll have to find what works for you and your boutique here, but you should start first with the clientele of your business. Where else is your target market shopping, getting their hair or nails done or even just enjoying a night out? Remember, as long as you have the same demographic as the business you want to team up with, it should be a successful event!

Once you have specific places determined that might work, then it's your turn to reach out and get connected with the people that own those businesses. Create a proposal for an event, whether it be a Sip and Shop or a holiday party, and suggest a date and time to the business owner you'd like to team up with. Make sure it works for both of you and advertise like crazy. This gives you an opportunity to cross promote. Maybe you run a discount for people who have made a purchase in the open business that night? Or there is a special door prize or raffle for the event where you can give away a gift card or a product package? Make this is the kind of event where both businesses will benefit. You will bring customers and they will have a designated space for you to park. If you can find the right people to attend, this partnership should be something that you do multiple times a year!

Focused Shopping: Private Parties

One of the biggest worries for a mobile retailer is regarding where to park. Opening up your boutique to private parties is the perfect solution. Whether it's an evening party at a customer's house, a lunchtime visit to a corporate office, or a school fundraising event, private parties are events that feature your truck as the main attraction.

It all starts with a host. Finding people to host your truck can be as simple as advertising in your truck, on social media and your website. Let the public know they can have the truck come to their home or office for a private event. Getting the word out is the first step to having hosts step forward. Once you've done a few private events, the attendees of those events will get excited and go ahead and contact you to host their own events.

Before you start booking parties, think about all the details, major and minor. Establish a "free travel zone." How far will you travel for free? If you have to travel over a certain mileage, charge a gas fee. There is no certainty you will be profitable at any event. But if you've already spent more than average on gas, then you want to at least make sure that cost is covered. How many people would you require to be at an event to make it worthwhile for you to attend? Also, does the host have adequate space for you to park? Is it flat enough for your vehicle to park without suffering on a slope? These questions are important to have thought through, as each will severely impact the success of your event.

Once you've been contacted, set a date and time with the host as soon as you can. It's important to listen to what will work for the group that's hosting. Perhaps a school event will need to be held after school hours, and maybe a group of women will want to have a ladies night out on a Thursday night at one woman's house. Most often, Wednesday to Friday nights will be the preferred times, but being open will ensure you maximize your bookings.

You'll want to communicate with the host, making totally sure they are comfortable with the idea of bringing you to their event. Having a standard invitation that you can customize for each party makes it easier for the host to send out invitations to guests. Getting closer to the date of the party, follow up and make sure that the host has plenty of guests ready to show up and shop! You might want to also ask if the guest have any special requests for items. You will, of course, have a wide array of products, but perhaps the guests will tap into something that's timely and you can purchase for the boutique.

What does the host get out of having you come to their event? First and foremost, they have the pleasure of supporting a new small business that's not only innovative, but can pull up in the space they desire! It's important to never charge the host for coming (unless they are outside the travel zone that you've established). With parties, you are crossing over into the direct sales realm. Direct selling companies never charge for hosts to sell in homes. In fact, they give the hostess free gifts or discounts on their purchases that night. It would be advantageous of you to duplicate this model and offer your host a discount on product and/or free gifts for having you. Often, a host will end up spending the most money. Most hosts are such big fans of what you are doing that they will go so far as to host you at an event! Reward them for inviting friends, feeding them and cleaning up the house! You want to treat every host like gold. The goal is to get them to become a repeat host. Whether it's once a month or once a year, repeat hosts should be increasingly rewarded for continuing to support your business by hosting parties.

Determining Your Host Incentive Program

If you've ever been to or hosted a direct selling business party, you know that hosts receive incentives for hosting. Whether it's money towards purchasing more product or a discount on the product they purchase, this concept is a standard practice amongst many businesses. It's important when you are determining your incentive program to think about a few things:

1. What can you afford to offer as a discount? Think about doing a % not $ off.
2. Sliding scales are great! The more the party makes, the more discount the host gets. Bigger parties are beneficial to everyone!
3. Consider special offers when times are slow.
4. The goal is to have repeat hosts. How can you up the discount or incentives when they host the second or third time?

Party Incentive Scale Example

TOTAL SALES DOLLARS	$300–600	$600–$1,000	$1,000+
Discount %	15%	25%	35%

THE ANATOMY OF A PRIVATE PARTY

- Arrive early, always. Give yourself plenty of time to get parked and get set up. No matter where you operate traffic is always a factor. If you arrive too early to head to the host's location, stop at a coffee shop to kill some time. Unless there is absolutely no way to avoid it, don't be late.

- Once you arrive, introduce yourself to the host and talk about where they were thought you could park. Make suggestions based on what you know works best for your business. This also provides you a quick moment to use the restroom if you've had a long drive!

- Let the host shop first, maybe even while you are finishing setting up. Put their items aside and have them check out at the end of the party. It provides a nice way to recap the party.

- During that recap, see if they want to host again! Maybe seasonally, or the next year. Try to make them a repeat host!

- Make sure you are accommodating to guests. If there are latecomers, be ok with staying past your planned stop time. You never know when that latecomer could be your biggest sale!

- Don't drink alcohol! Hosts might offer, but politely decline. You cannot appear to be drinking and driving, even if it is one glass of wine! You are running the store, not partying with guests.

- If you are at a home, stay out of the house as much as possible. The perk of hosting a mobile boutique is that you don't take over their house as other home parties do.

REAL LIFE STORIES

One summer, a woman contacted me about hosting a party at her home with The Fashion Truck. I had the date open, and it was in a nearby town, so of course, I said yes. A week before the event, I checked back in with her, and she told me that her friend who sold Stella and Dot would also be there selling her jewelry. My jewelry is similar to the style of Stella and Dot, but a lower price point since I'm selling directly to the customer, not via a representative. I asked the host if her friend knew I would be there. A day later she responded and said the friend knew, and she had requested I please take all my jewelry off the truck for the party. Seriously? I suggested that perhaps we reschedule for a different day since jewelry is at least half of my assortment and if I did that, I would have an awkwardly empty truck. Once I knew that this was the situation I figured I should just bow out, since both the host and the friend felt that this was an appropriate question to ask of me. Sometimes you have to turn down events if you don't think they are going to be right for you or your business.

Mobile Boutique Scheduling Final Notes

When you start your business, you really want to be open to anything and everything that will get you out on the streets and in public. Try events a couple of times and if you are making money, keep doing it! If you find an event isn't making you money, stop as soon as you can get out of it.

Since your goal with scheduling your time is to have consistent income, you'll want to be on the road as much as possible. Thursday through Sunday are notoriously the best days for retail. It's when people get paid, when they start to relax and think about things like shopping for pleasure. Try to maximize every weekend, even booking morning and night events on the same day if it's an option!

Vehicle Maintenance

Choosing a truck means you are now a truck driver! Truck drivers must be aware of new road signage and know the dimensions of their vehicle. They also must be fully aware of the maintenance schedule.

First, you need to know the height and length of your truck. This will help you know if you can fit under bridges, in garages and how much space you need to park.

Secondly, you'll need to know the Gross Vehicle Weight (GVW) of your truck. GVW is often measured in tons (t). One ton is 2,000 pounds. Make sure you have converted the weight into tons, as this is the metric used by road signs for going over bridges.

Subsequently, going over a bridge or through a toll booth, you need to know how many axles you have. This will be the basis for which you pay a toll and know what weight is correct for bridge driving.

Find a repair shop that fixes medium to heavy trucks in your area to do work on the moving parts of your truck. Oil changes and tire rotations need to happen every 5,000 miles to ensure you run smoothly. Check the levels of fluids regularly. This is something you can have your repair shop teach you how to do. You want to always keep an ear out while you are driving. Does something sound funny, or feel funny? Take it to the shop and get it checked out. Remember, the safety of your truck will allow you to be successful.

Frequently Asked Questions

There are some questions from new mobile boutique owners that seem to come up. For example, how do you go to the bathroom when you are out on the mobile boutique? Well, planning is a huge part of it. On your drive, drink what you need to feel hydrated. Go to the bathroom before you open up. Then, make sure you don't drink too much during the first couple hours at an event. If your event is four hours long, start drinking again at two hours in. It's all up to you. How close are the bathrooms and how long can you last? If an emergency comes up and you really need to use the restroom, just close your doors and go quickly. If you are at an event that you can trust a neighbor, ask them to watch over your area, or tell people not to go inside until you are back. Don't dehydrate yourself if it's hot. Just plan ahead and know where the bathroom is.

Security of items on the vehicle, and loss prevention is also something new owners are concerned about. If you want, install cameras on the mobile boutique. Or, a classic way to ensure people stray from stealing is to communicate with them. From the minute they walk through the door, welcome them and talk to them. Most mobile boutiques are pretty small, so you should easily be able to keep an eye on the 8-10 people that will be in your vehicle. Staying aware and talking is the best way to prevent stealing. In terms of where to park your vehicle, make sure you have a safe spot, like a gated storage space or even your driveway. Check with local zoning laws, most of the time mobile boutiques under 15,000 pounds will be ok to park in a residential driveway. Of course sweetening up the neighbors with a gift and asking also helps!

When setting up your mobile boutique, make sure there are items and signage outside of it. Whether you have painted your back doors with chalkboard paint, or have a sandwich board, make sure you have a welcoming entrance where people can browse a bit of merchandise outside and feel comfortable coming in. Remember when you were young and your parents told you to stay away from strangers in vans? Well, this idea sticks around in adulthood and getting the modern adult to jump in a vehicle full of merchandise can take a bit of work. Warming them up outside, keeping it bright and airy with fun music on the inside can absolutely get people to come up the stairs! Keep in mind, you will always have "peekers" who just want to look in from the outside to see what's going on and then walk away. Don't worry about them; they probably aren't your ideal customers anyway! ▨

BOUTIQUE NOTES:

CHAPTER TWELVE

WHAT NOW?

At this point, you should have a pretty good idea of what kind of boutique you want to open, where you might want to be located, and a handle on what it takes to get to your opening day. Now it's time to set some goals for you and your business.

Perhaps you've finished reading this book, and you feel overwhelmed or can not imagine yourself in a boutique setting right away. The idea of putting all that money out with no return in sight scares you. That's ok! Start slow. Maybe you purchase some inventory and do some local events with a tent and table set up. That will only cost you between $500-$1,000 to start up. Maybe that leads to doing some home parties with your inventory. Awesome! Starting small, testing products, learning about your customer better…all of this is good stuff. From this book, you know all of the basics to being a merchant- how to make money buying and selling goods. You could even create a business Facebook page or Instagram account and start selling via photos and shipping to customers. Just because this book is about starting a boutique, doesn't mean you need to dive head first into it. Take small steps and build your business from the ground up!

I've included some worksheets in the appendix for you to use in starting and growing your boutique. Use these to brainstorm, write notes and also set goals. Start thinking about your "why." Why do you want to start a business and open a boutique? Lifestyle freedom? Flexible hours? Having something that is your own? Expressing your creativity? Great! All of these are amazing reasons to open a boutique, and you'll want to go back to your WHY every time you have a hard day. There will be hard days, months, years even. Owning your own business is hard work and requires serious determination. You will have to grow tough skin and have an open mind. As the economy changes, the weather changes, your customer base changes, you will have to shake, rattle and roll to adapt what and how you do things in your business to stay moving in a forward direction always. Think about the concept of 1% change. Changing 1% may mean redoing a window display, or advertising with a more local newspaper, or inviting Girl Scout troops to host a meeting at your store. Those 1% changes each day, week and month can add up to huge changes in the course of a year or two. Imagine there is a day that no one comes through the front door. That might be a hard day for you, since you'll think traffic has stopped. But it hasn't! Use that time to redesign your visual displays, or get caught up on accounting or social media posts. Maybe you even just spend the day cleaning. You will be prepared for the next days when people will start coming again. Owning a business is like surfing; when you catch a wave, it feels awesome, and you never want it to never end. But the wave inevitably does, and you will have to paddle back out to catch the next one. Knowing there is the next wave out there is what keeps your spirits up. If you can ride the waves, always knowing in your heart that you are doing the best you possibly can, success is bound to come your way. ▨

APPENDIX

Helpful Worksheets

Define Your Market Worksheet 112

Retail Pricing Worksheet 114

Brick and Mortar vs. Mobile Boutique Pros/Cons List 116

Where to Purchase Products 118

Resource Links 120

Define Your Target Market

What is your target market's age, gender, income, location?

In one sentence, define who your target market is:

Where does your target market live?

Where does your target market shop?

What is the kind of products your target market want to buy?

What prices is your target market willing to pay for those items?

RETAIL PRICING WORKSHEET

Arm yourself with this sheet when you finally go shopping for products for your boutique!

ITEM	BASIC RETAIL PRICE

$$\text{Initial Margin \%} = \frac{(\text{Retail Price} - \text{Wholesale Cost})}{\text{Retail Price}}$$

BASIC WHOLESALE COST	FASHION RETAIL PRICE	FASHION WHOLESALE PRICE

Pros and Cons List
BRICK AND MORTAR

*Fill out the pros and cons for opening a Brick and Mortar store
then compare with your Mobile Boutique list*

PROS	CONS

Pros and Cons List
MOBILE BOUTIQUE

*Fill out the pros and cons for opening a Mobile Boutique
then compare with your Brick and Mortar store list*

PROS	CONS

Where to Purchase Products

TRADE SHOWS FOR APPAREL, ACCESSORIES AND GIFTS

NEW YORK
Fame: www.fameshows.com
MODA: www.modamanhattan.com
Accessories the Show: www.accessoriestheshow.com
NY Gift Show: www.nynow.com

ATLANTA
AmericasMart: www.americasmart.com

DALLAS
Market Center: www.dallasmarketcenter.com

CHICAGO
StyleMax: www.stylemaxonline.com

LAS VEGAS
Magic: www.magiconline.com
Project: www.magiconline.com/project-las-vegas

MARKETS/SHOWROOMS FOR APPAREL, ACCESSORIES AND GIFTS

NEW YORK
Stores on 6th Ave/Broadway/7th Ave between 30-40th Streets

ATLANTA
AmericasMart Atlanta: www.americasmart.com

DALLAS
Dallas Market Center: www.dallasmarketcenter.com

CHICAGO
The Merchandise Mart: www.mmart.com

LOS ANGELES

San Pedro Mart: www.sanpedromart.com
California Market Center: www.californiamarketcenter.com
New Mart: www.newmart.net
Cooper Design Space: www.cooperdesignspace.com
LA Mart: www.lamart.com

ONLINE RESOURCES

LA Showroom: www.lashowroom.com
Fashion Go: www.fashiongo.net

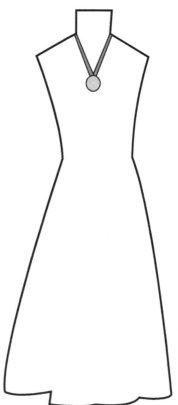

Resource Links

BRANDING AND DESIGN
  Logo & Graphic Design:
  www.Emery-Creative.com
  www.Elance.com

WEBSITES:
  www.Squarespace.com
  Shopify Free Trial: bit.ly/emilyshopify
  www.Storenvy.com
  www.Wix.com
  www.Weebly.com

SOCIAL MEDIA:
  www.Fortheloveofyourbiz.com
  www.Facebook.com
  www.Instagram.com
  www.Twitter.com
  www.Pinterest.com
  www.LinkedIn.com
  www.GooglePlus.com
  www.YouTube.com
  www.Mailchimp.com

BOUTIQUE SET UP
  Federal Employee Identification Number:
  http://www.irs.gov/Businesses/Small-Businesses-&-Self-Employed/
  How-to-Apply-for-an-EIN

CREDIT CARD PROCESSING:
  www.GoPayment.com
  www.Square.com
  www.Paypal.com

ONLINE ACCOUNTING SOFTWARE:
www.Quickbooks.com

POINT OF SALE SYSTEMS:
www.Vend.com
www.NCRSilver.com
www.Shopify.com

STORE FIXTURES AND PAPER GOODS:
www.Ikea.com
www.StoreSupplyWarehouse.com
www.GemsOnDisplay.com
www.Uline.com

MOBILE BOUTIQUE SPECIFICS:
www.HondaGenerators.com
www.AmericanMRA.com
www.Stepvans.com
www.Craigslist.org

FINAL NOTES

Did you enjoy this book? Great! Stay in touch with what's up with Emily on her Facebook page:
www.facebook.com/StylishandSuccessful

Subscribe to Emily's YouTube Channel and get deeper trainings and tutorials: bit.ly/emilyyoutube

Reviews are gold to authors! If you've enjoyed this book, would you consider rating it and reviewing it on Amazon? Here's the link to do that: bit.ly/boutiquehandbook

Want to join a community of like-minded boutique owners? Join Emily's free group The Fashion Truck Tribe here: bit.ly/trucktribe

CPSIA information can be obtained
at www.ICGtesting.com
Printed in the USA
BVHW04s1154110718
521390BV00028B/1132/P